Fairies

Adult Coloring Book

Life is full of things that stress us out. Between work, children, bills, and chores at home, our minds are inundated with stuff vying for our attention. Coloring is a great way to relax and allow stress to melt away.

Have a problem you are trying to figure out? Just open up this book, take your colored pencils, and begin filling in the blank spaces. Don't focus on anything, but coloring what is within this book. By doing this, you will clear you mind, and just might come up with the solution you've been searching for.

With 30 illustrations and designs of fairies to color, this book has something for every skill level. So just take a moment, relax, and color.

You can tear this page out and use it to put between the images so as to avoid bleed through.

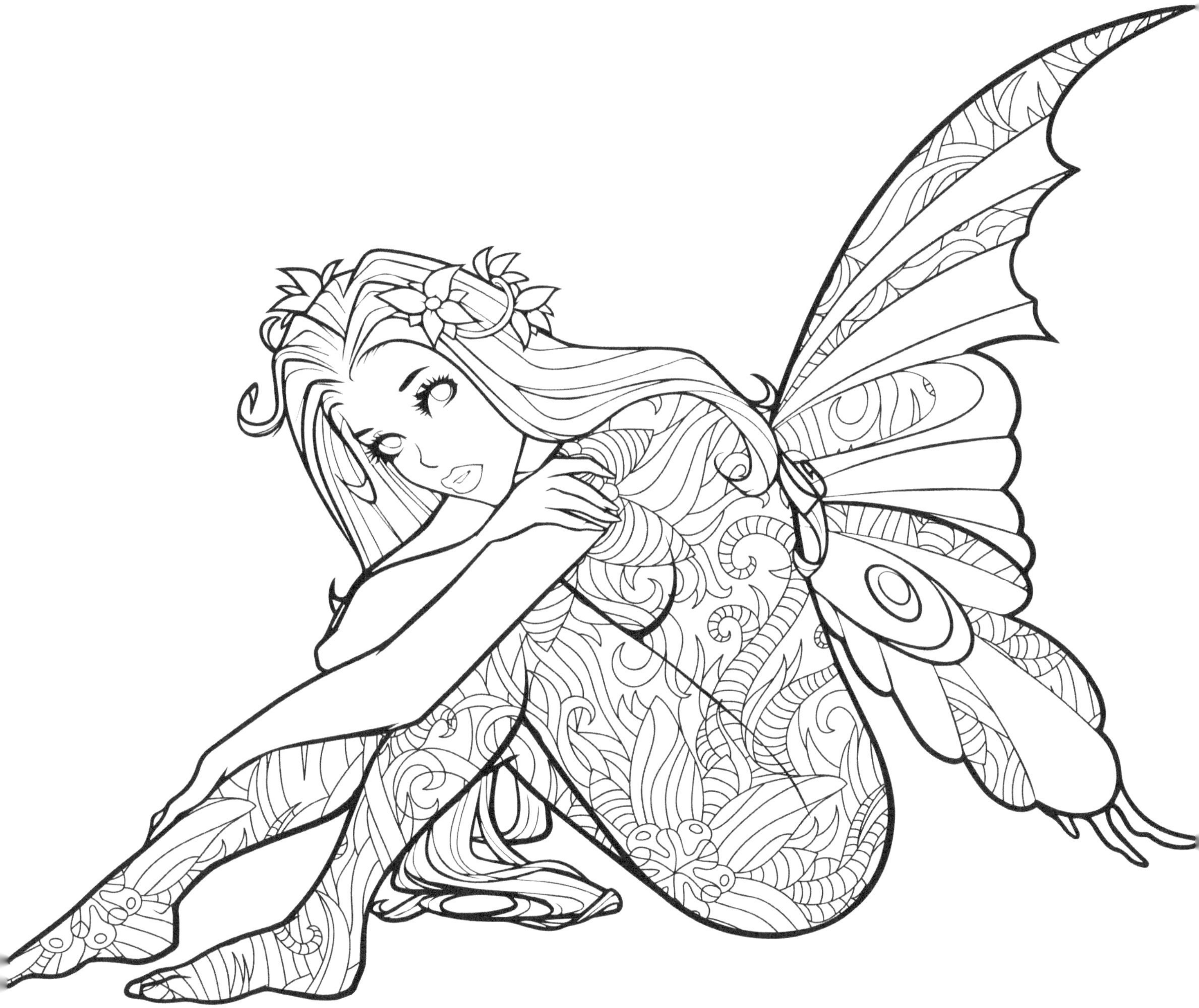

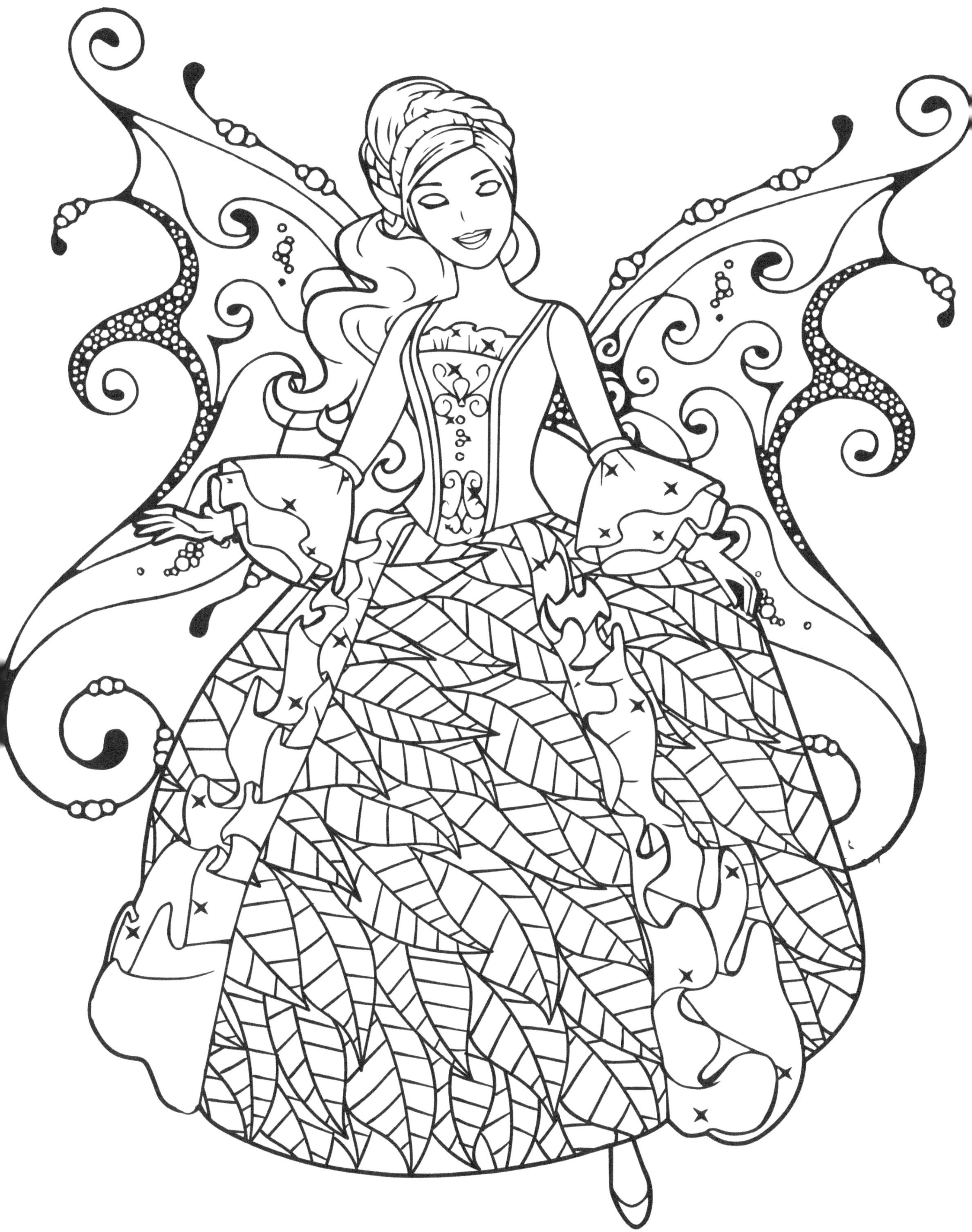

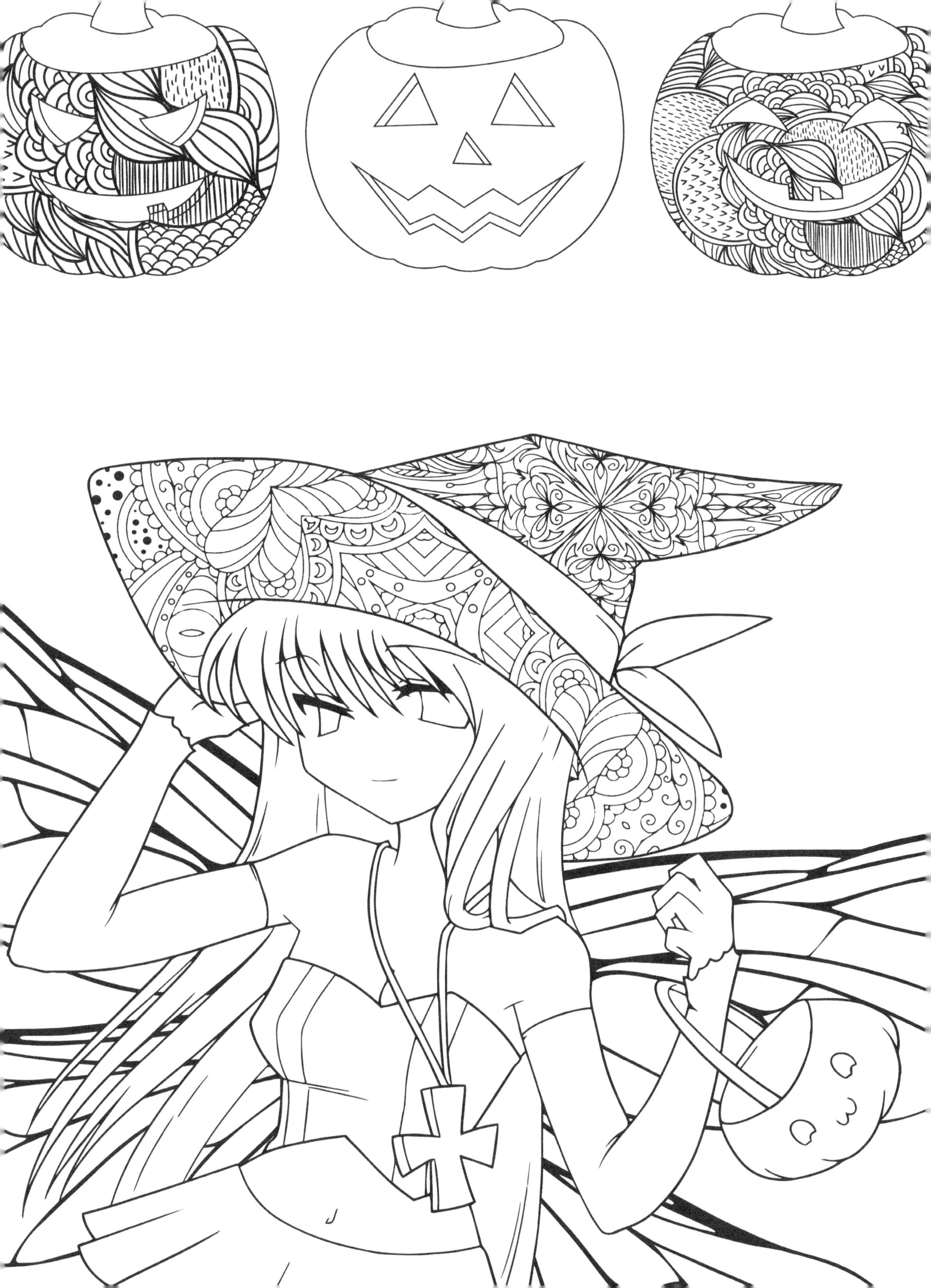

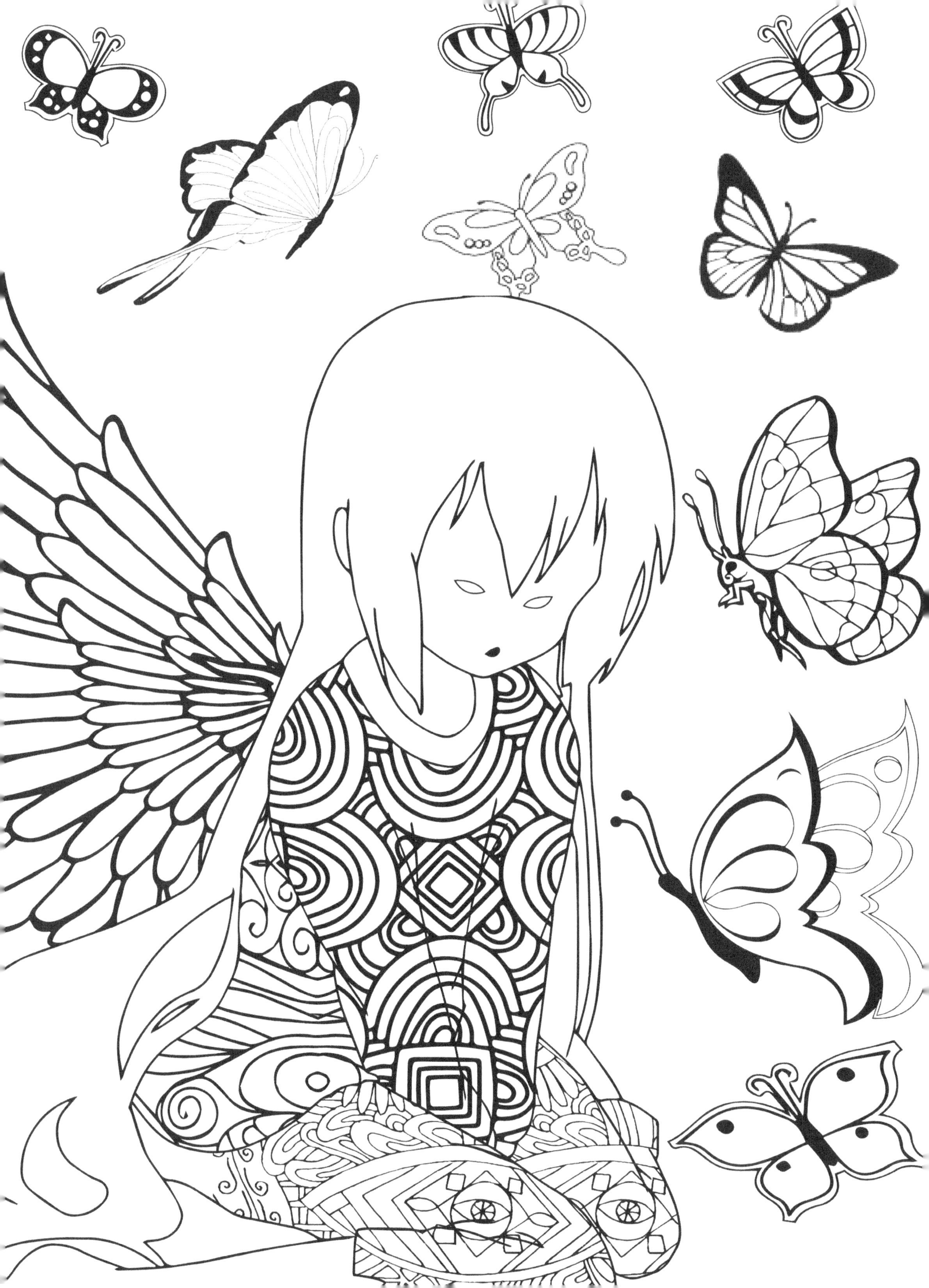

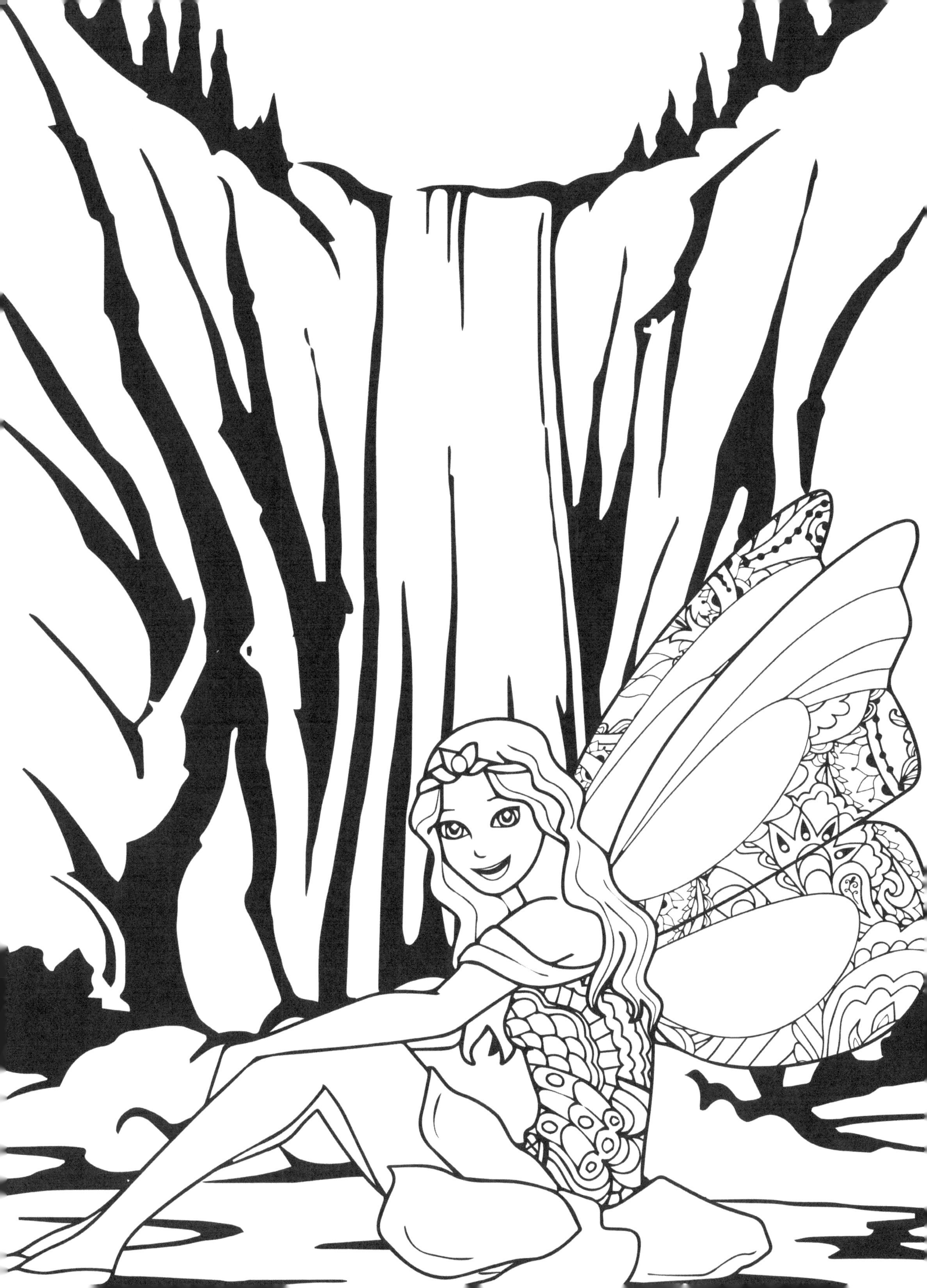

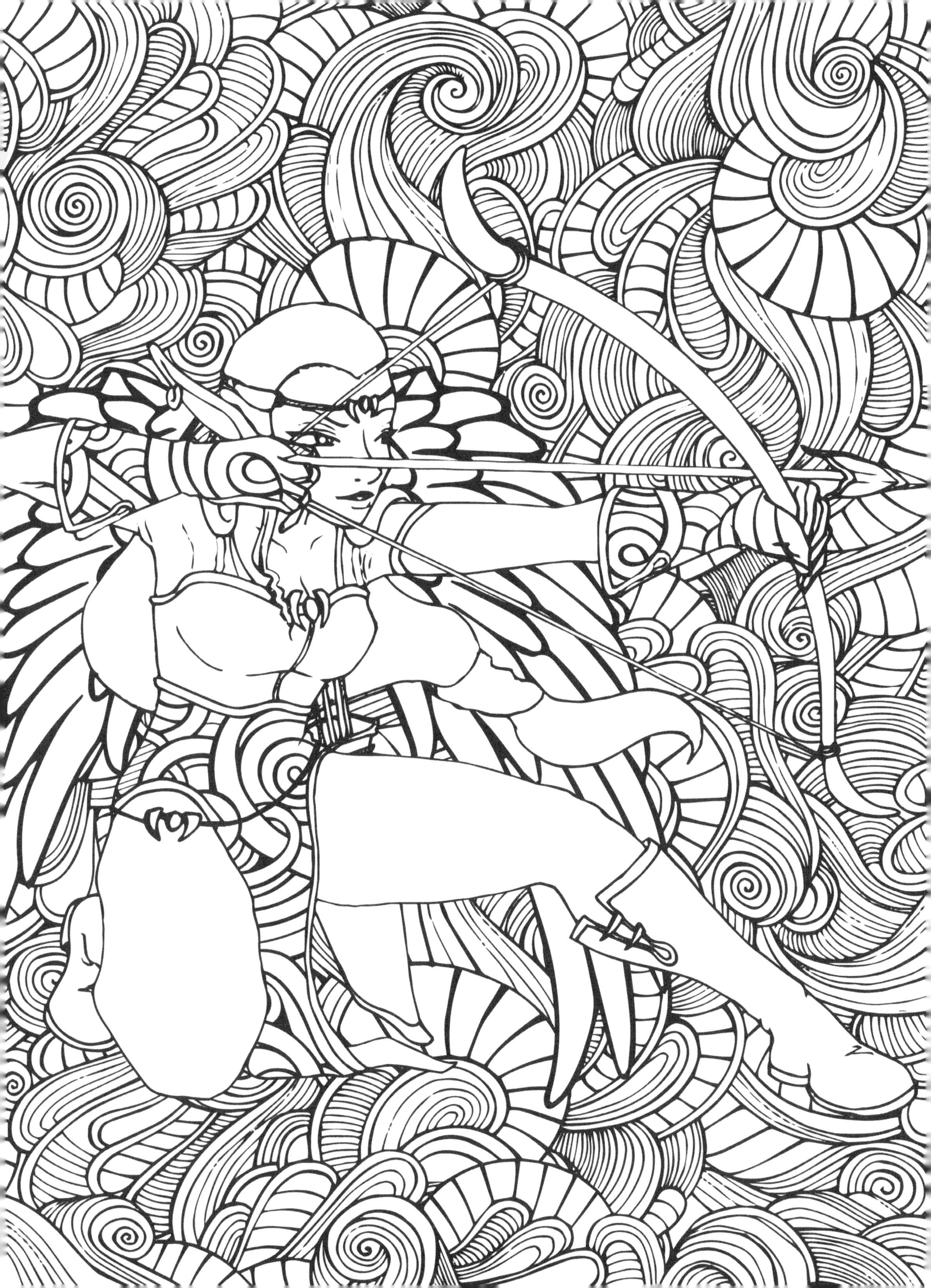

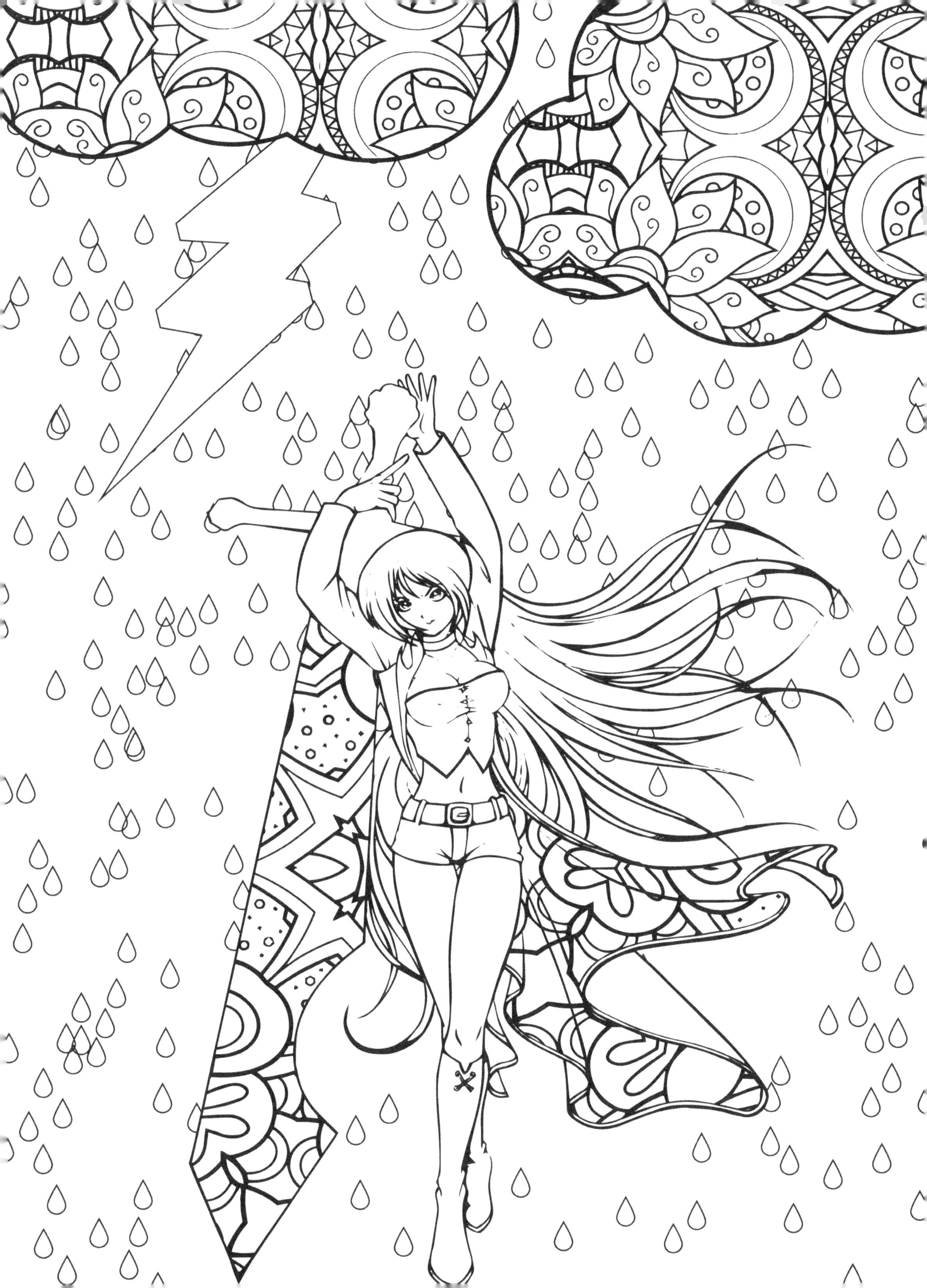

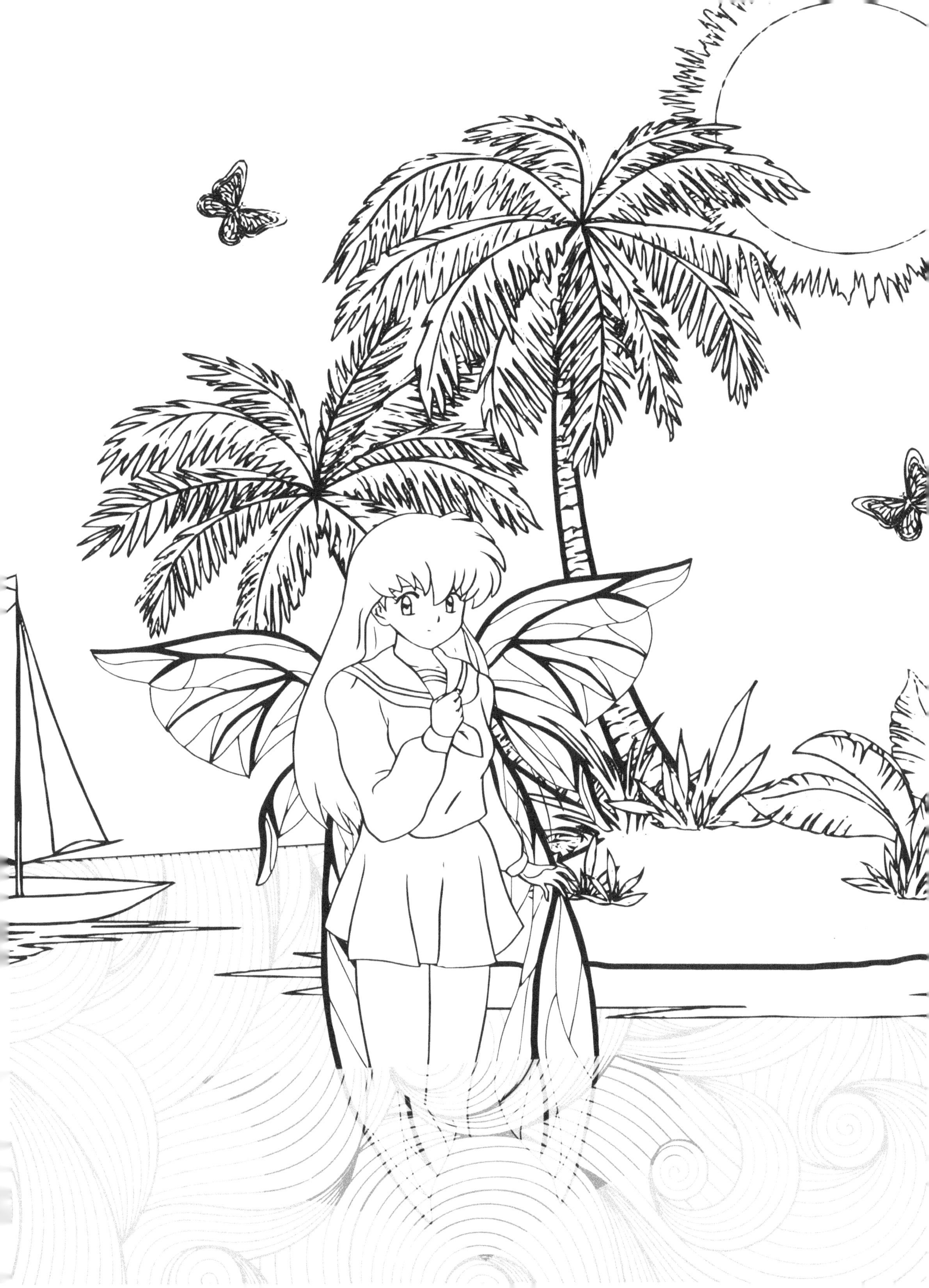

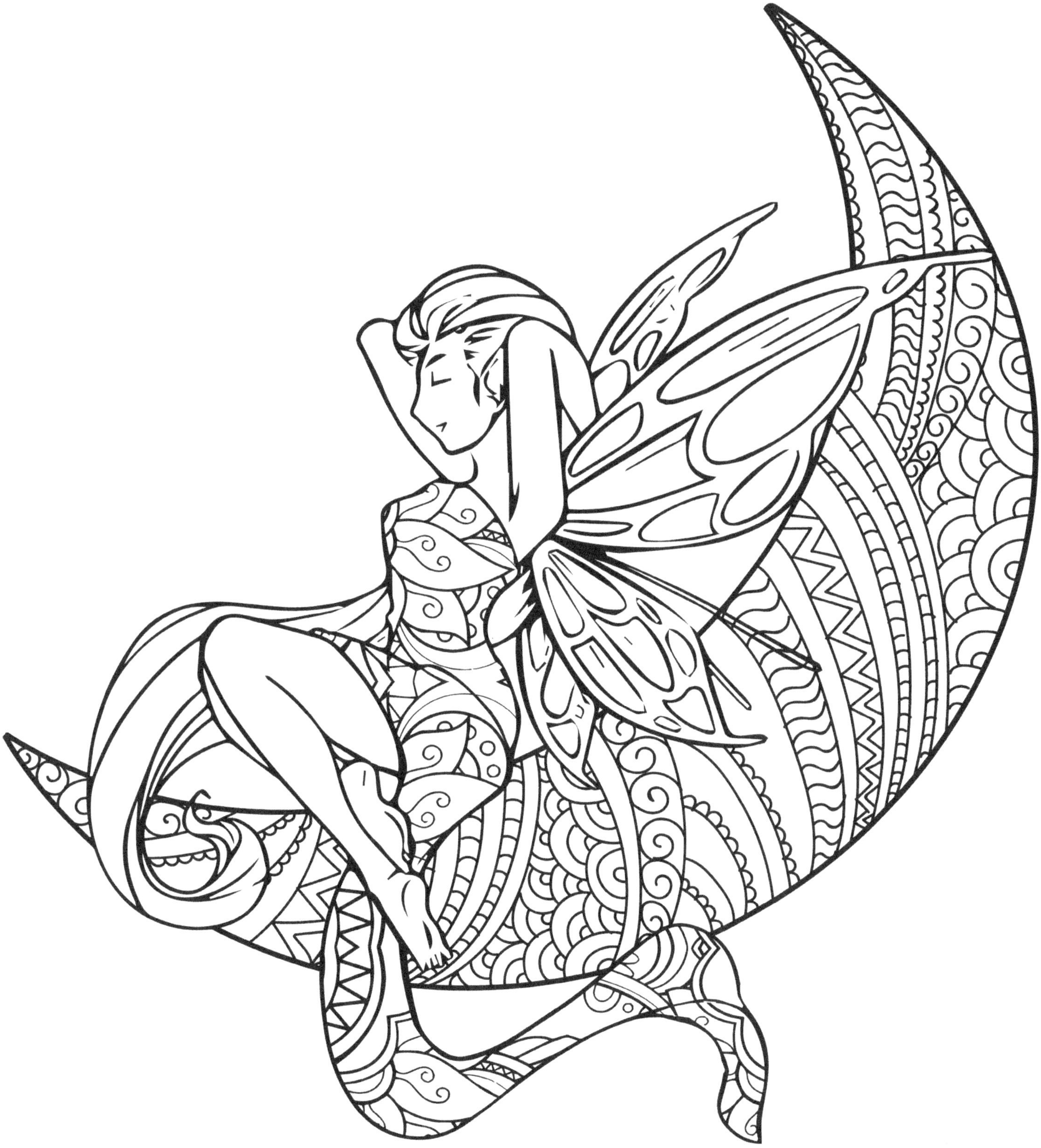

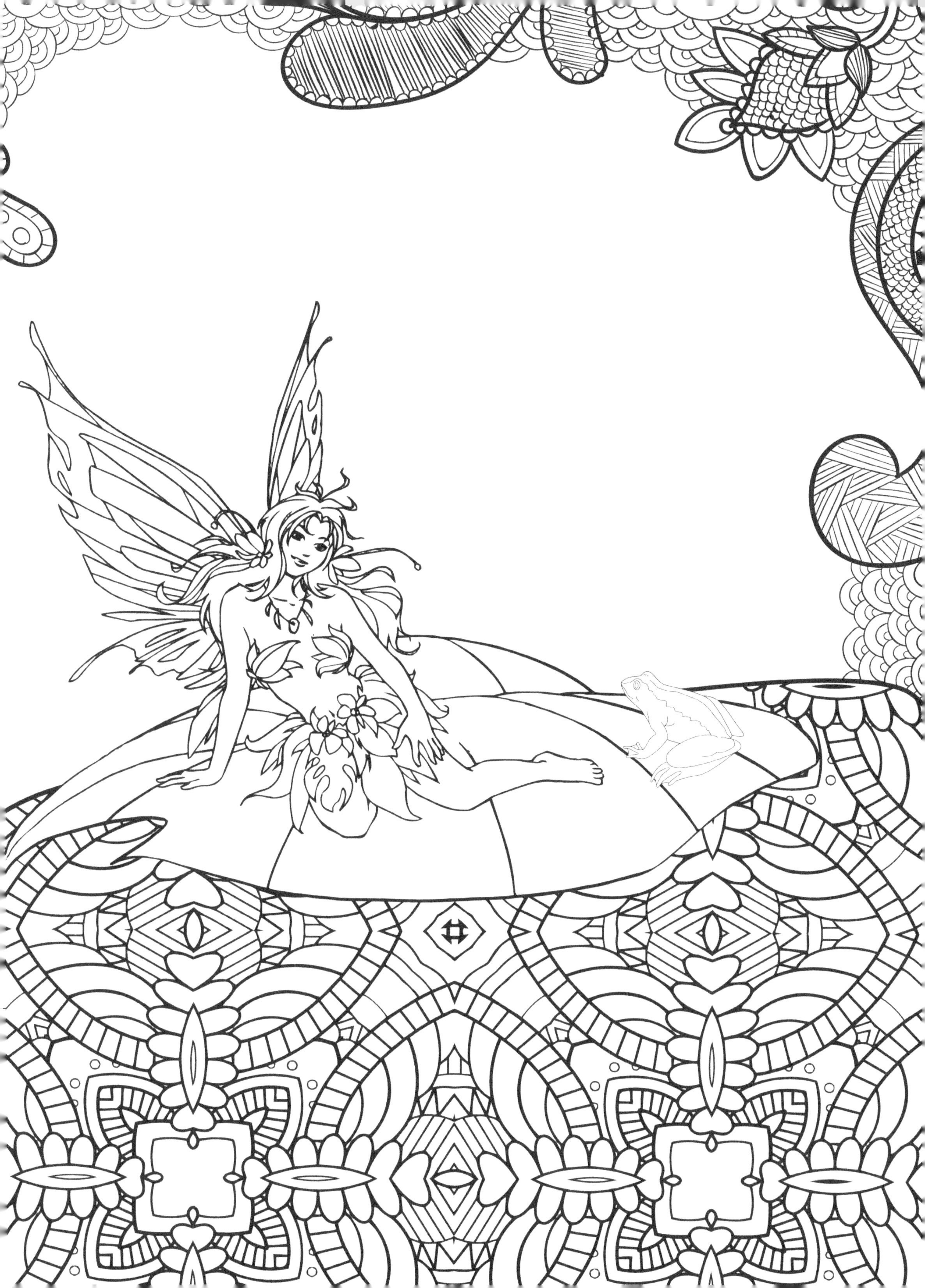

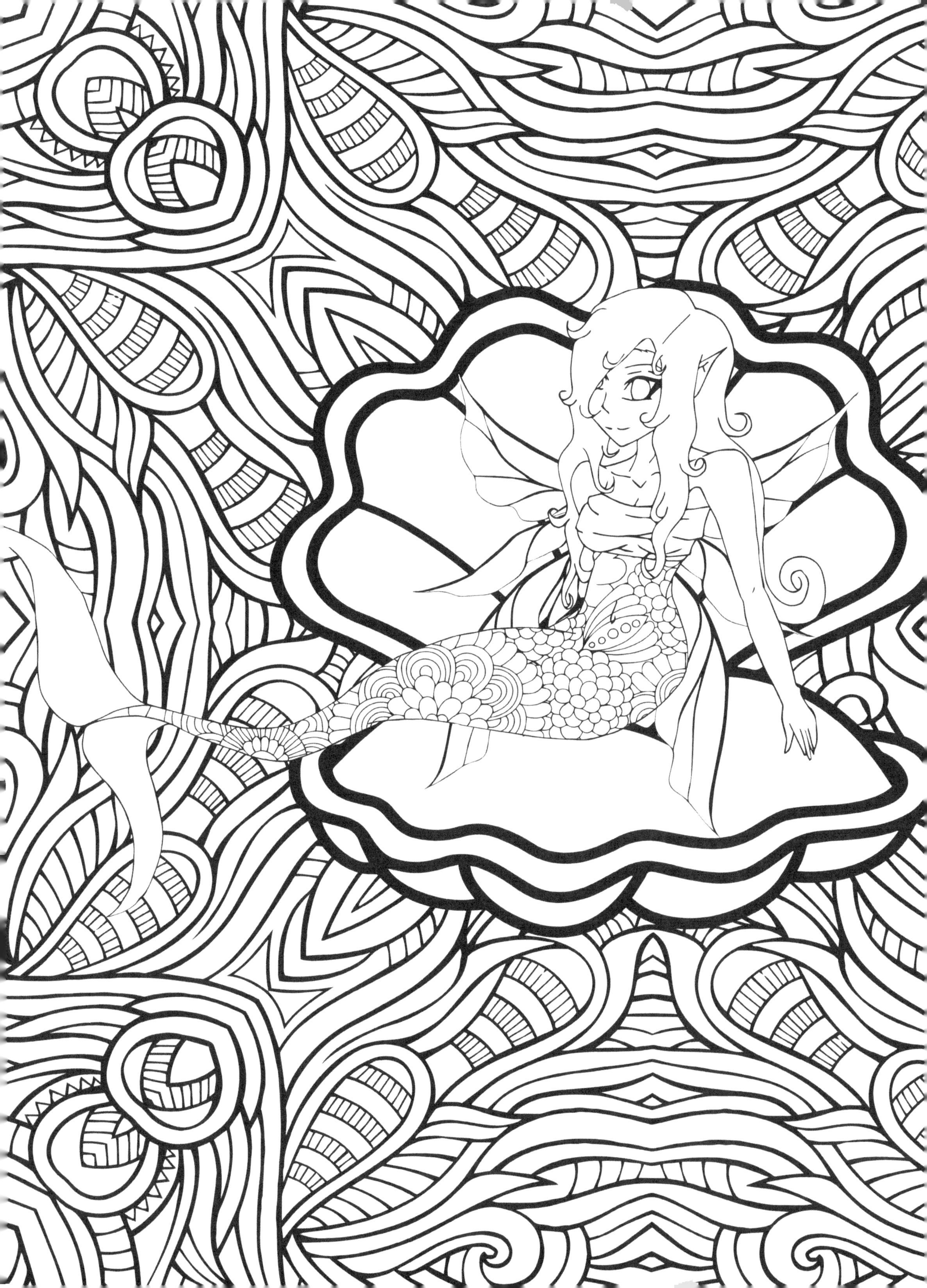

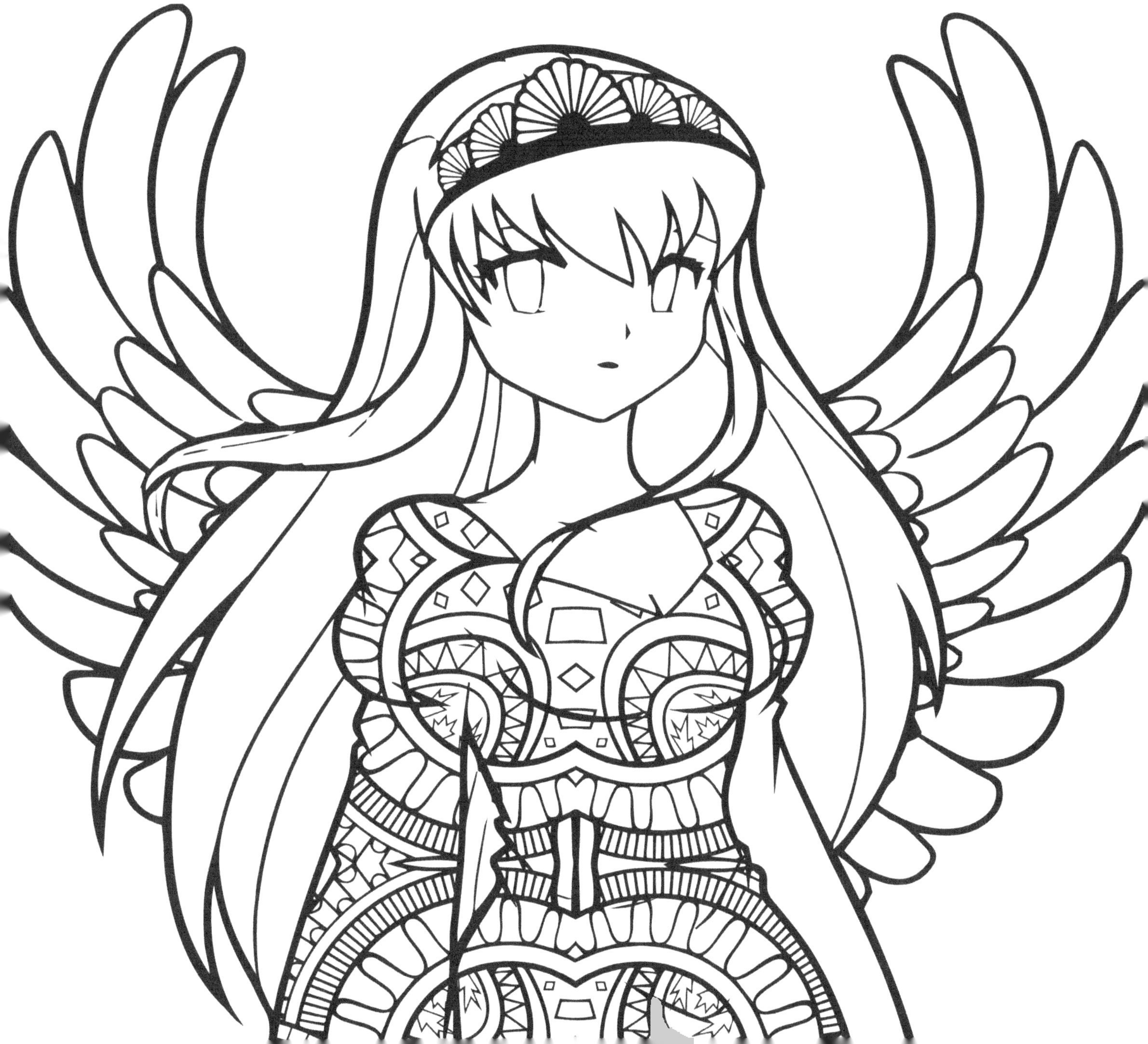

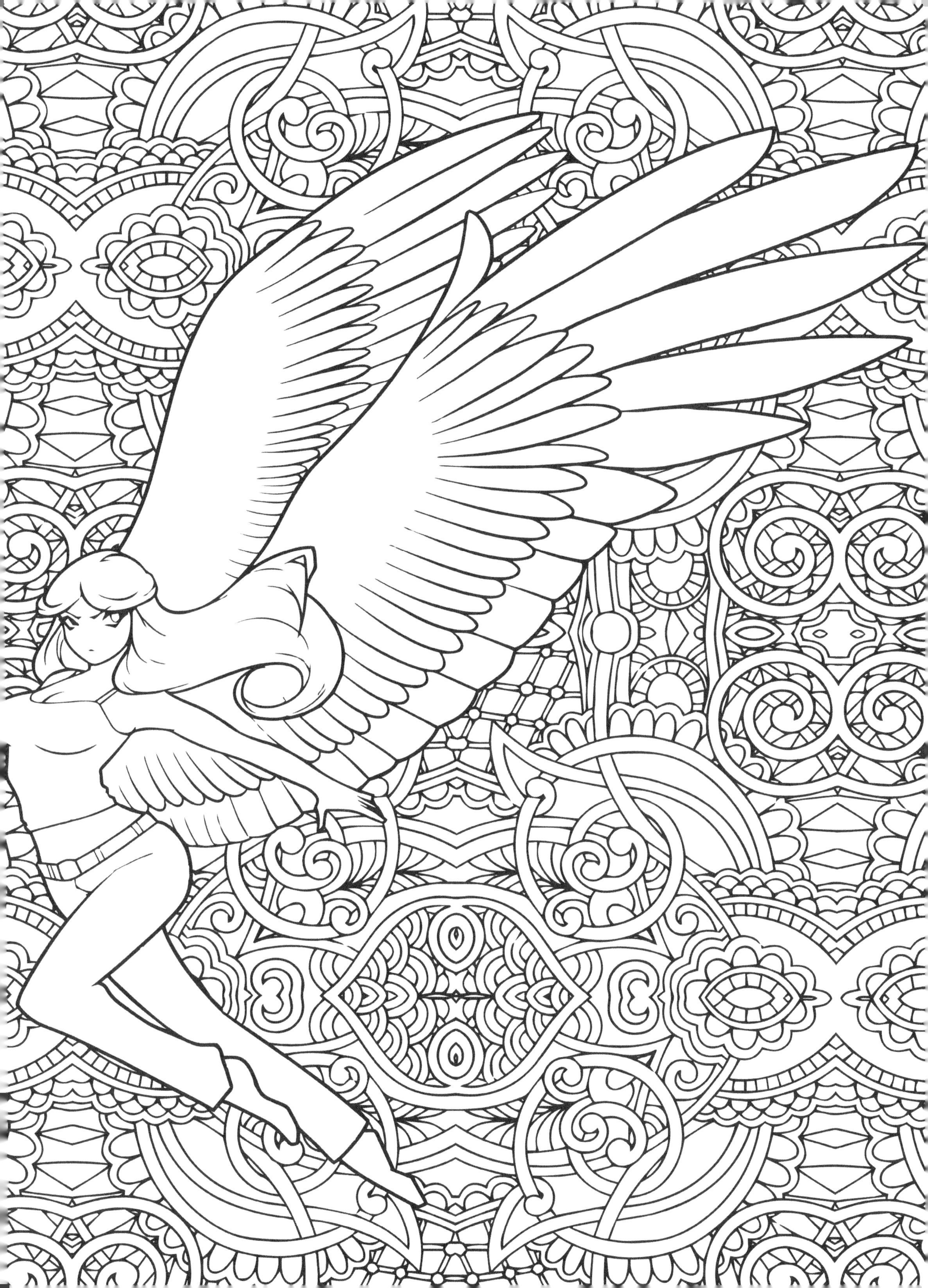

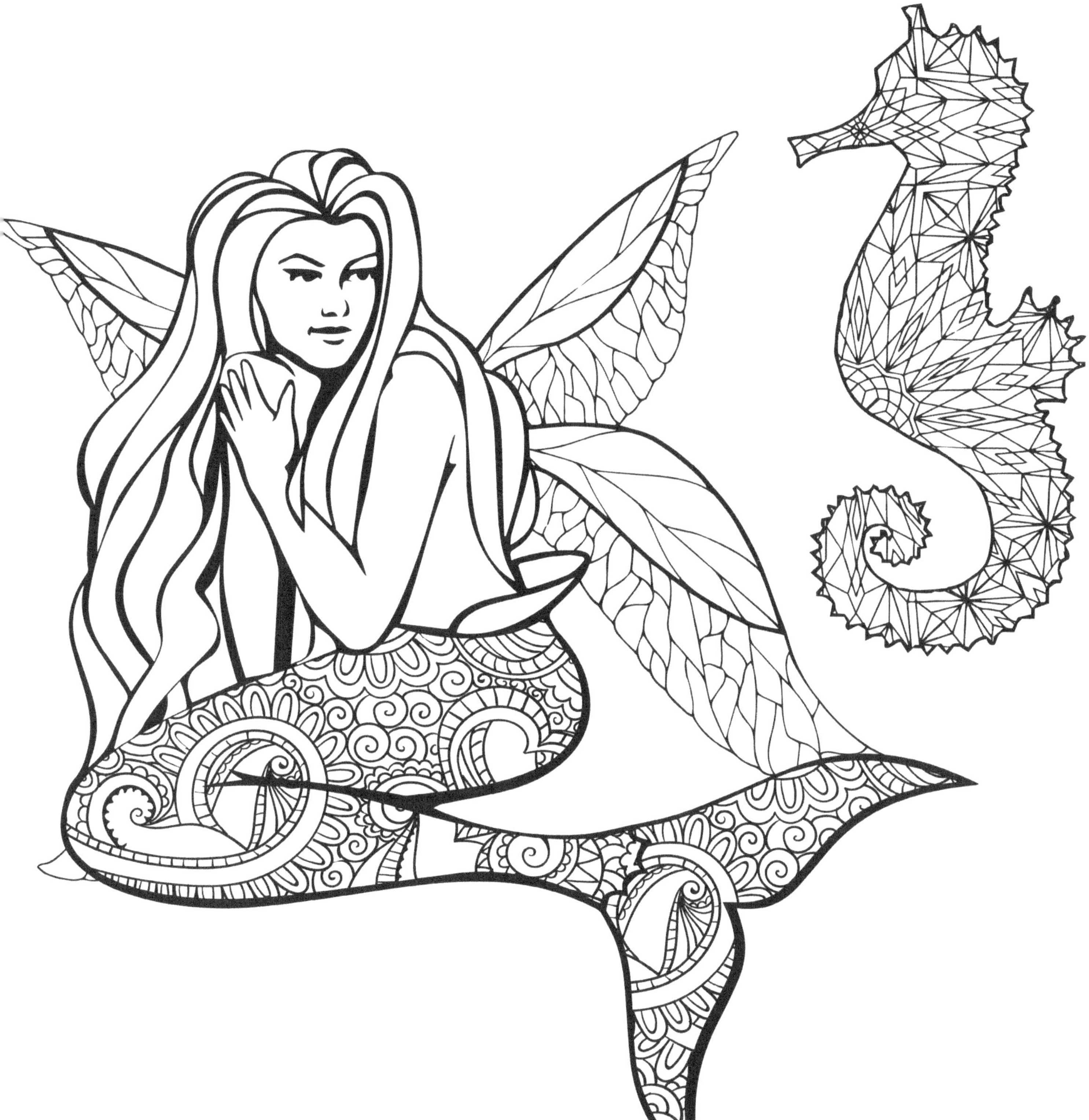

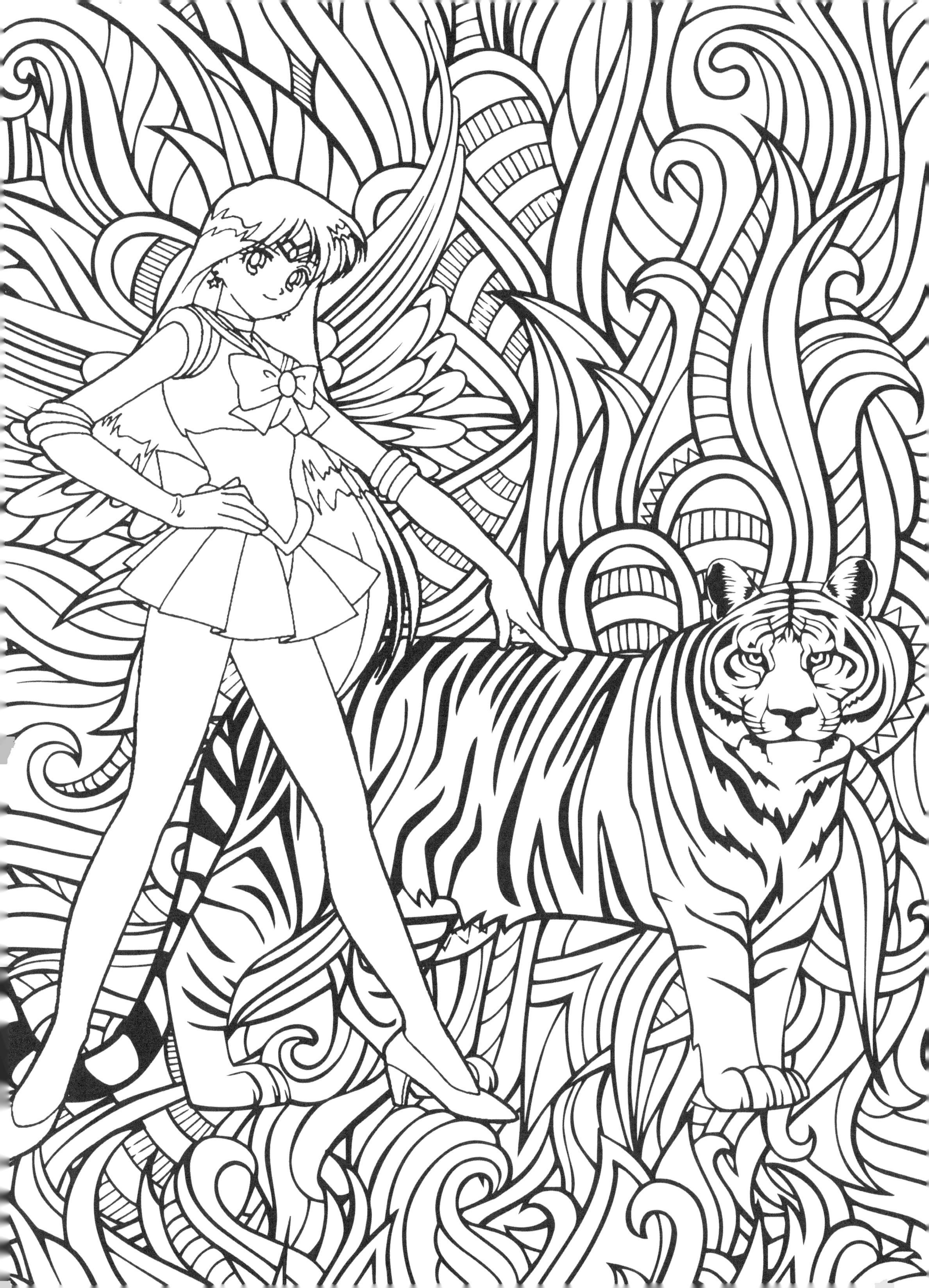

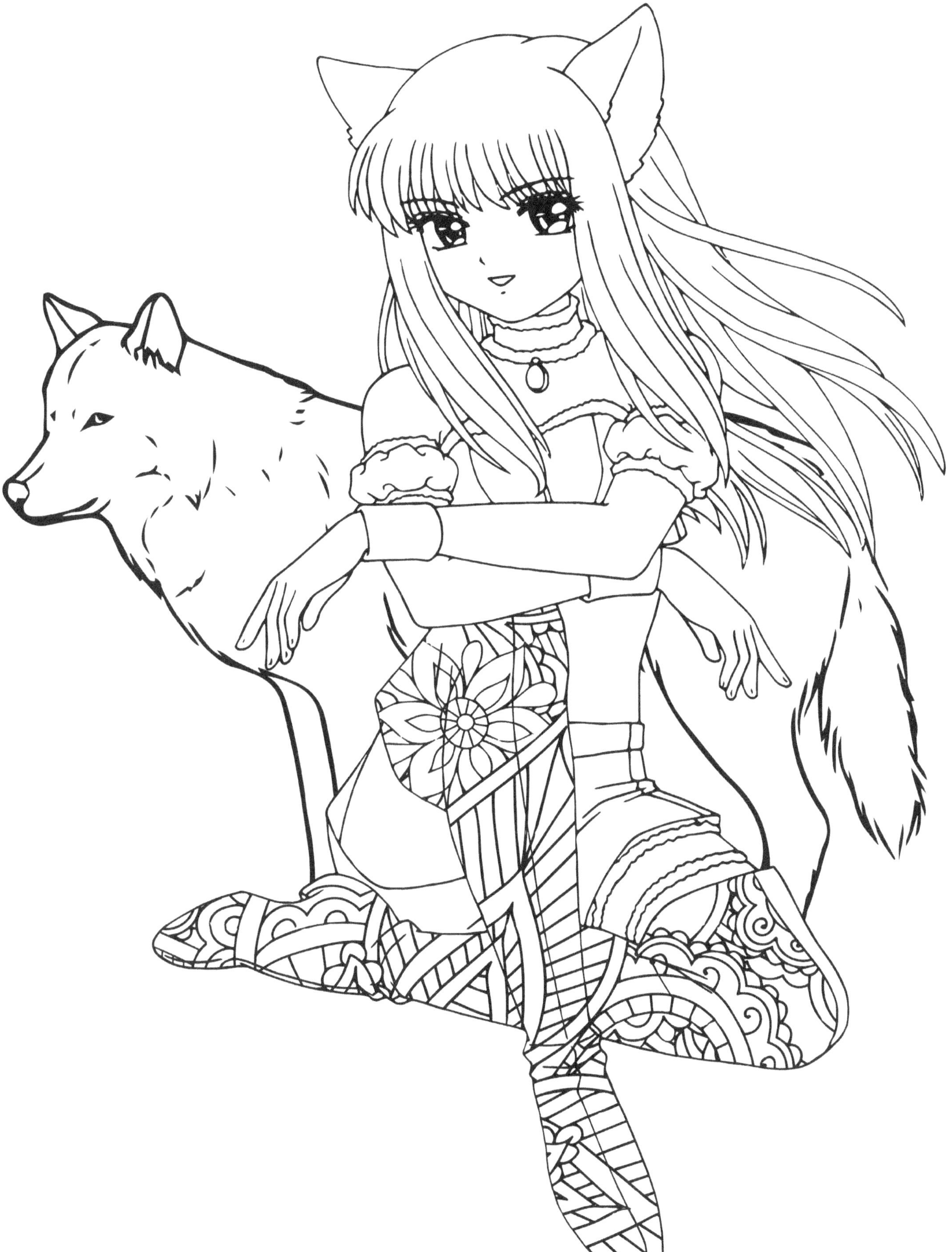

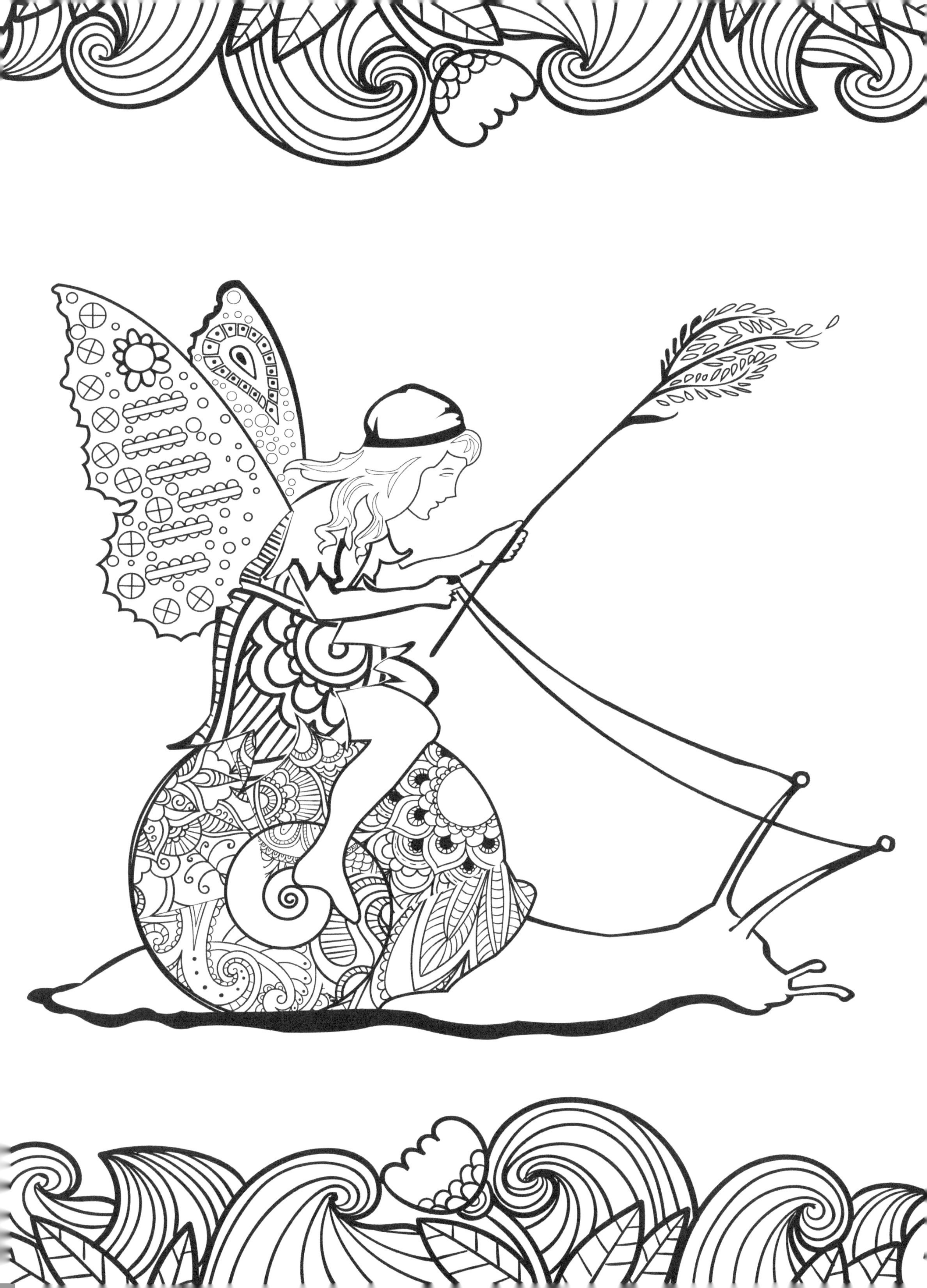

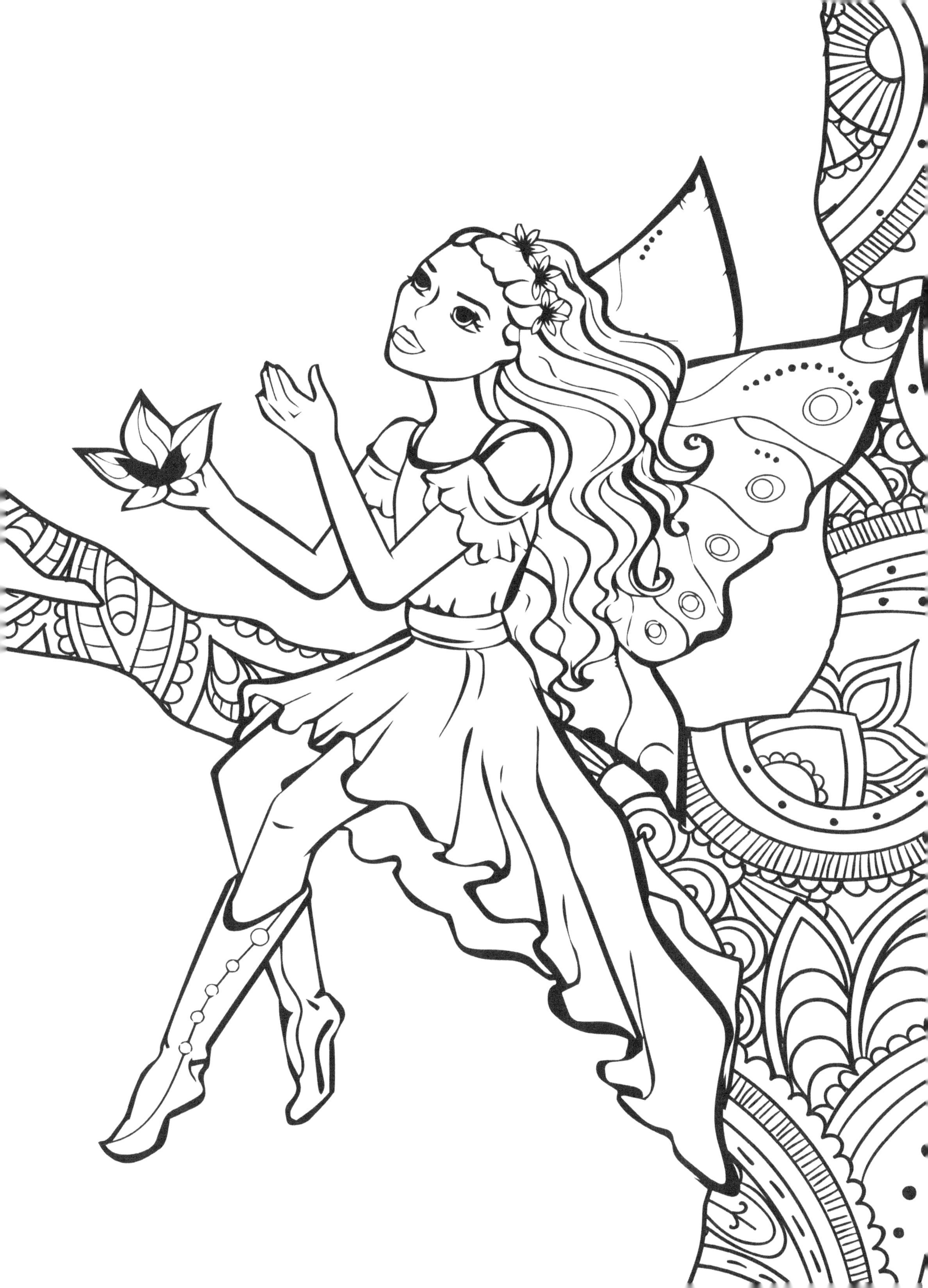

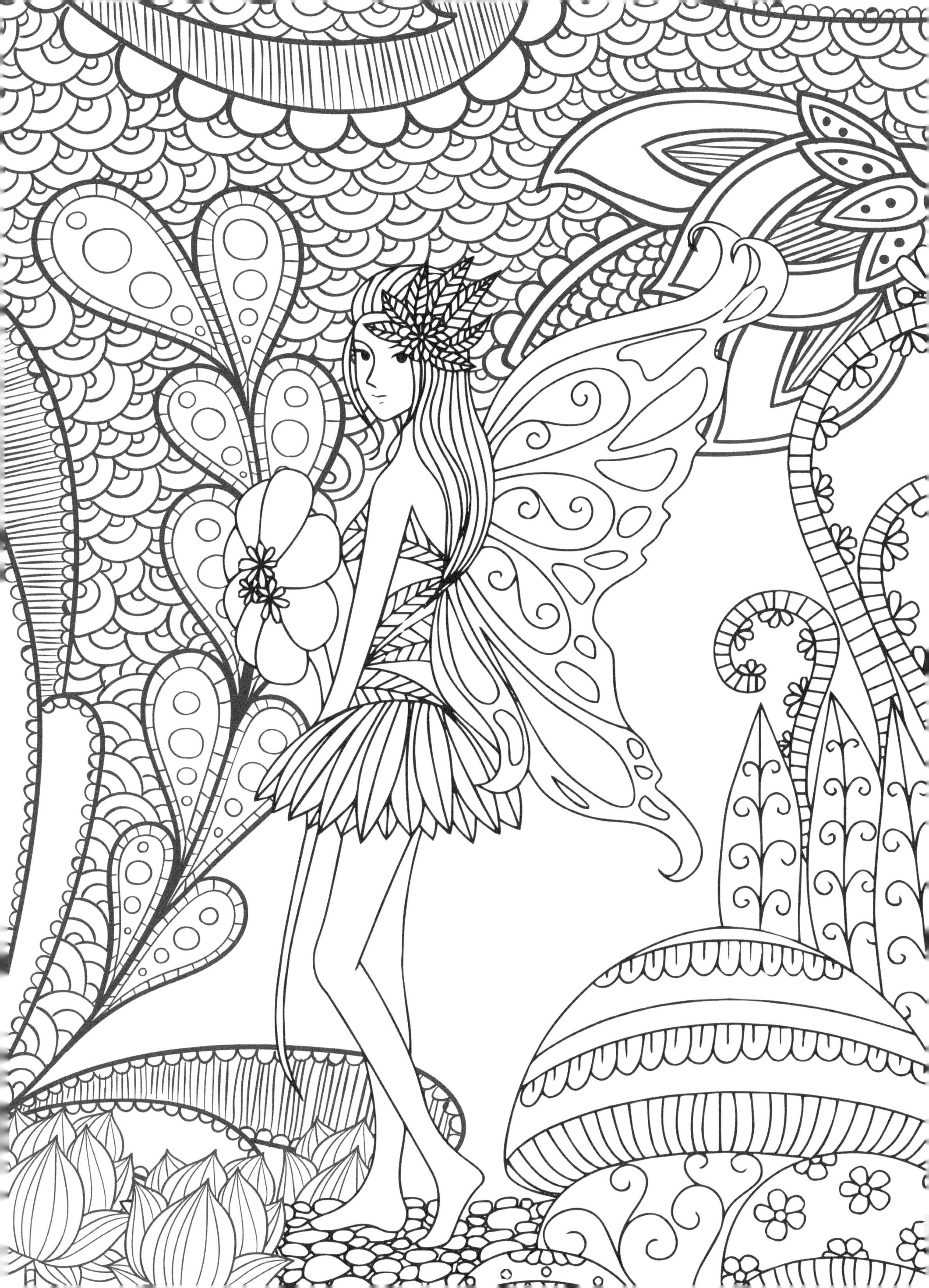

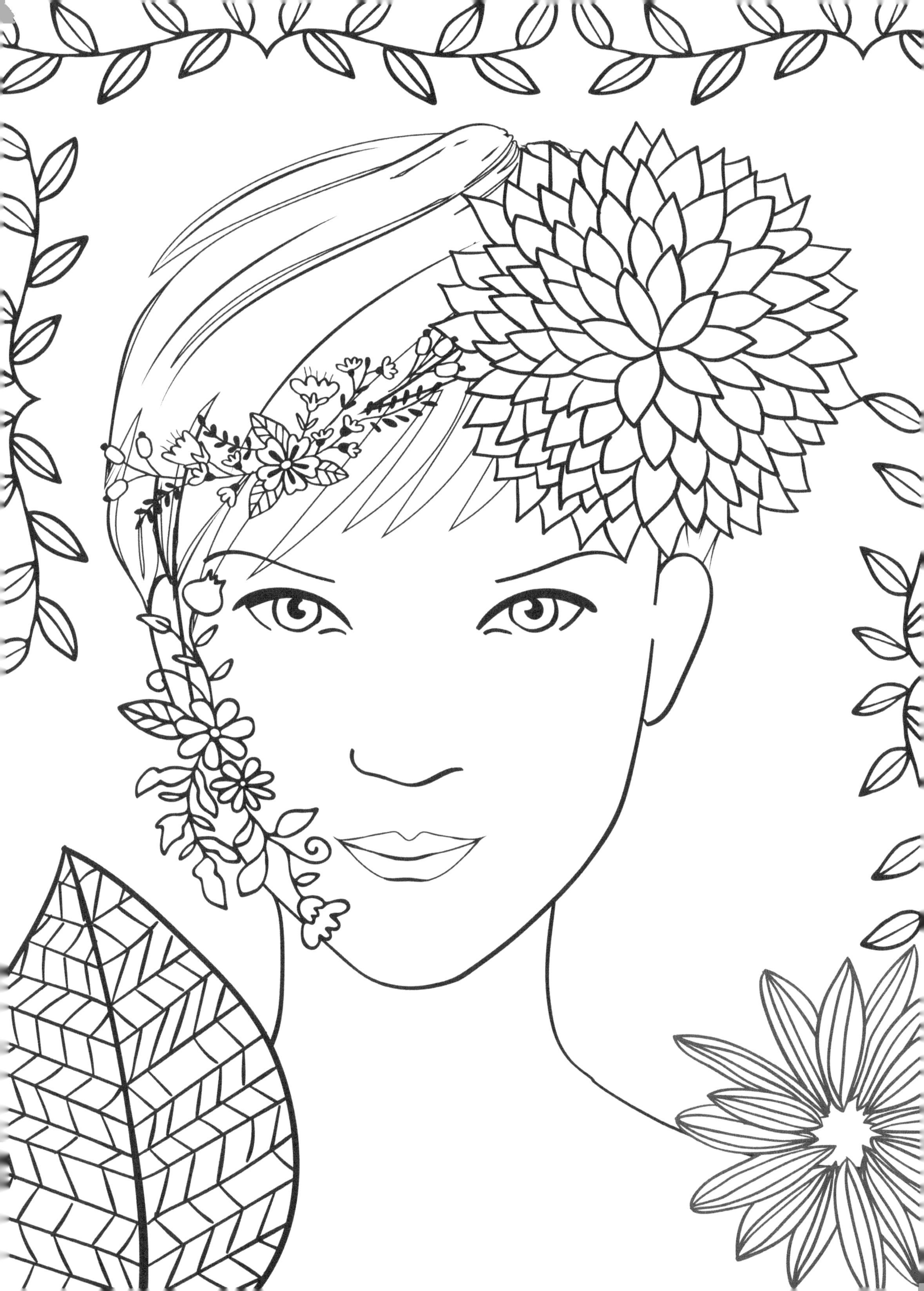

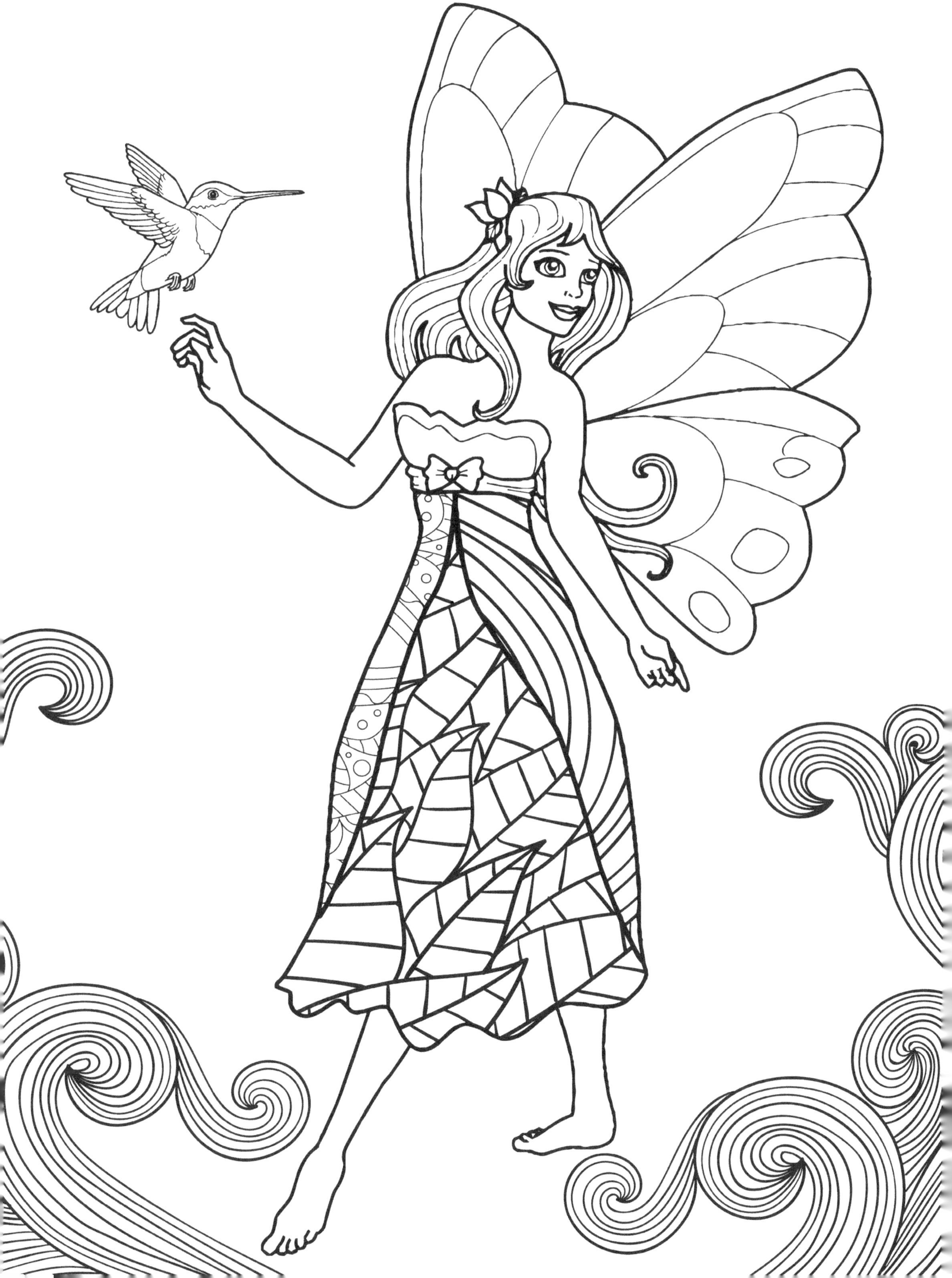

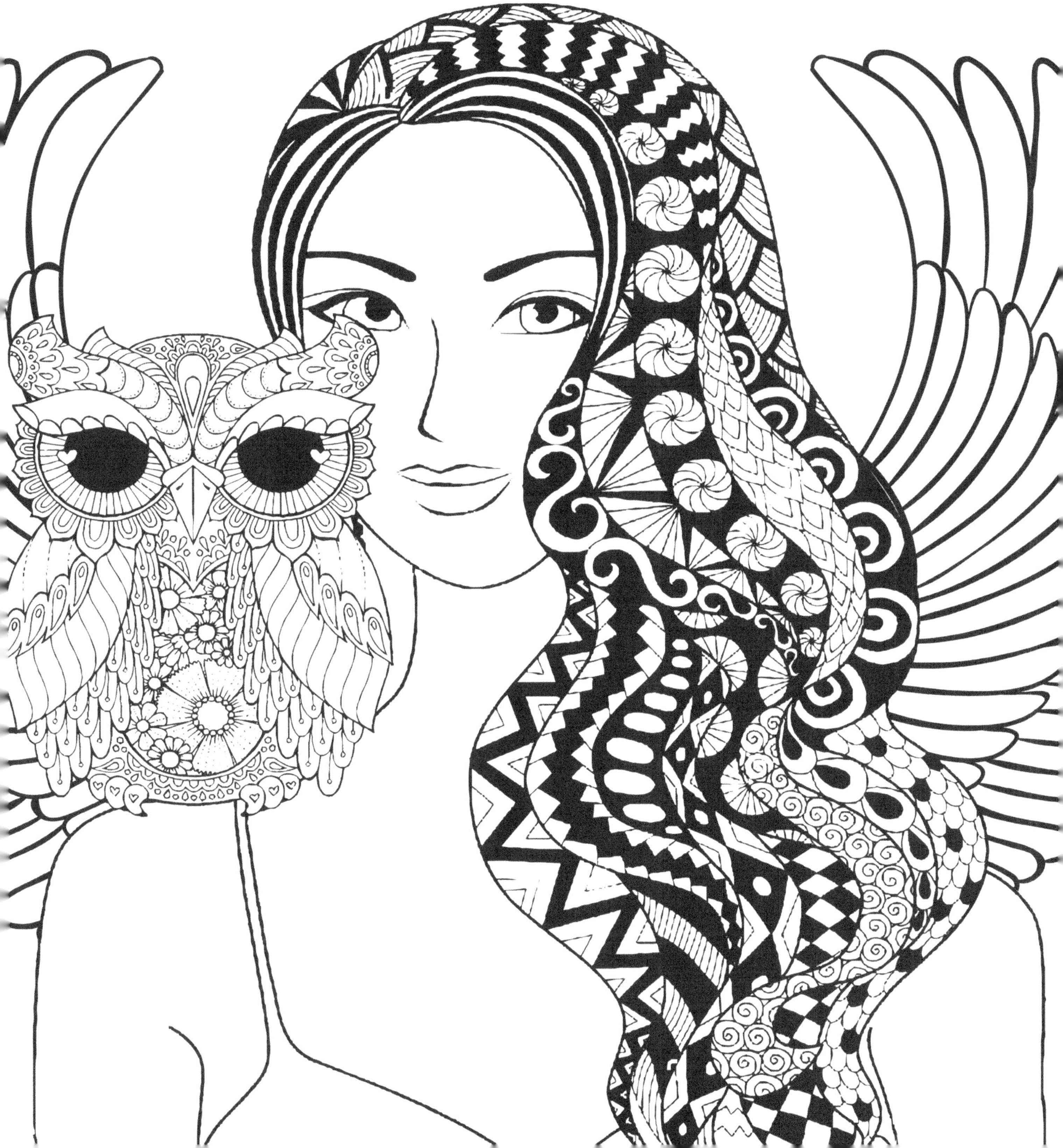

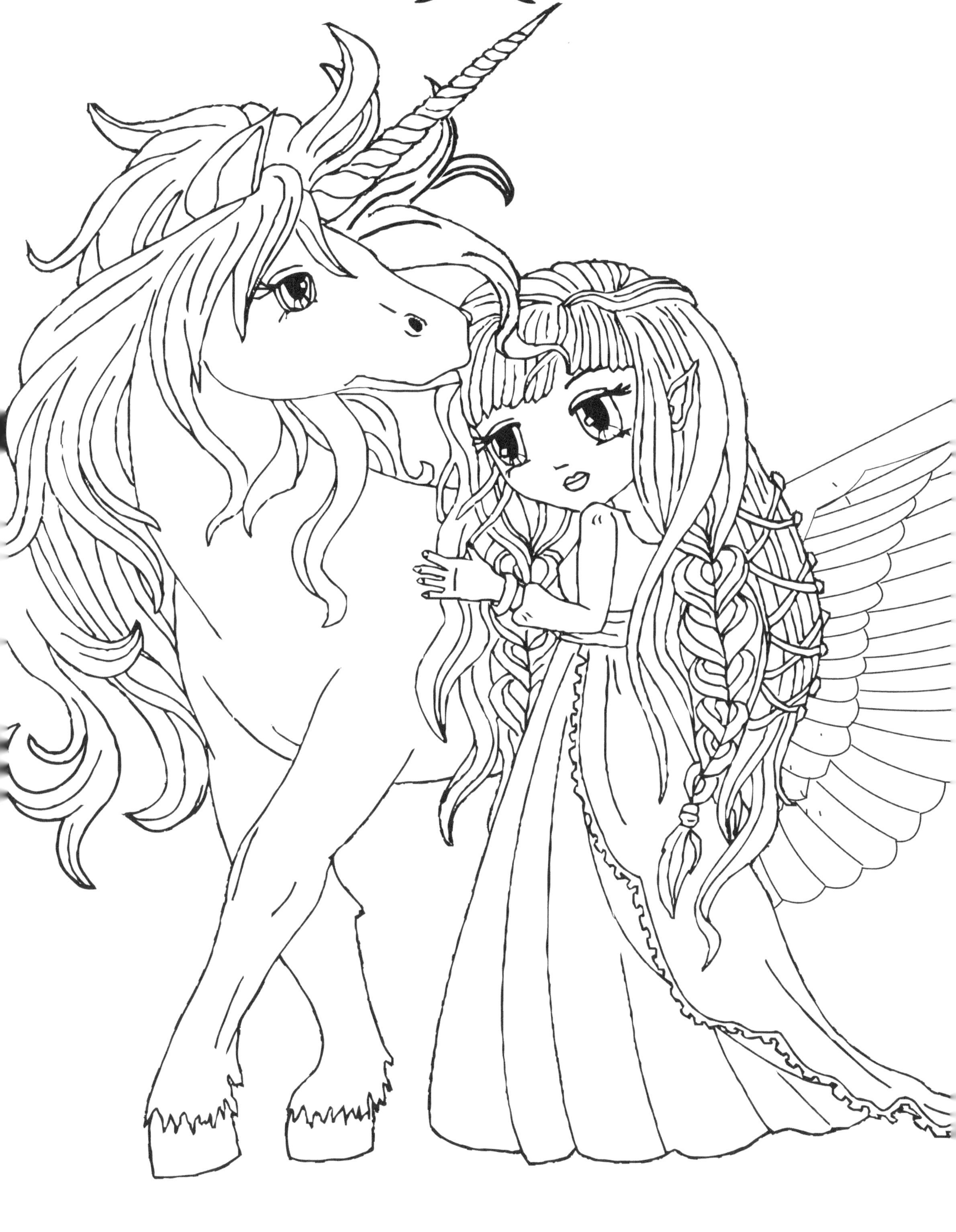

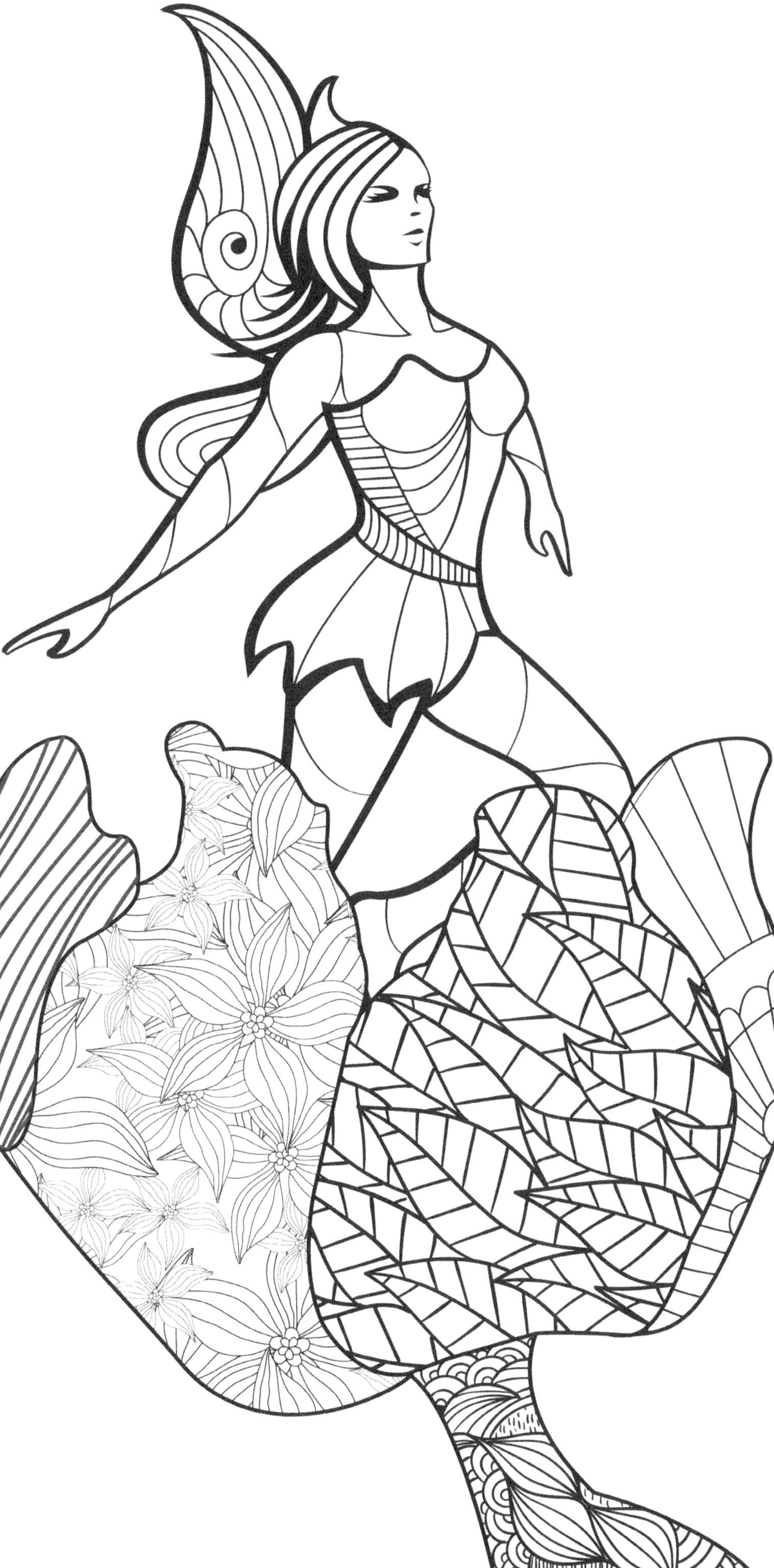

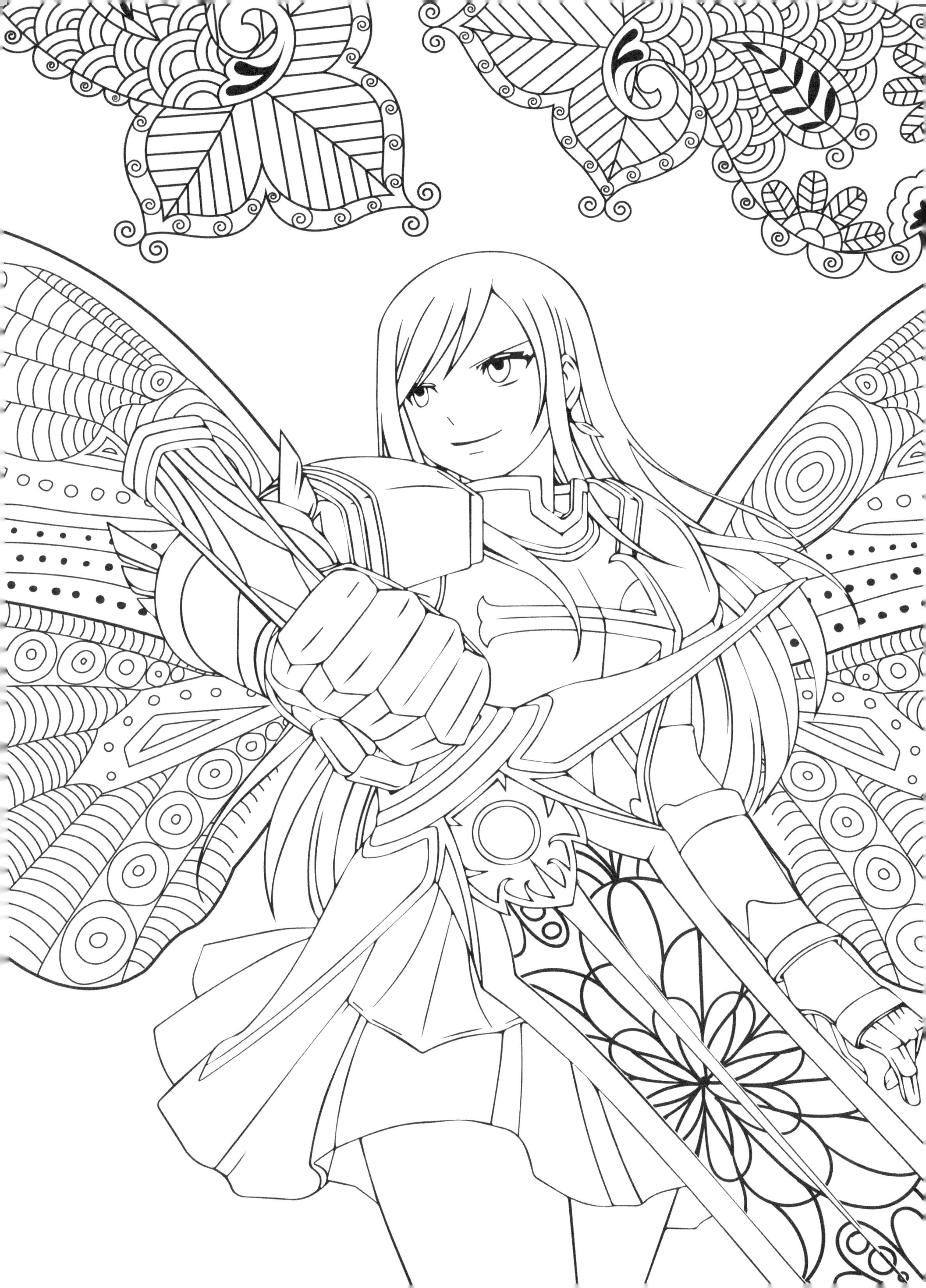

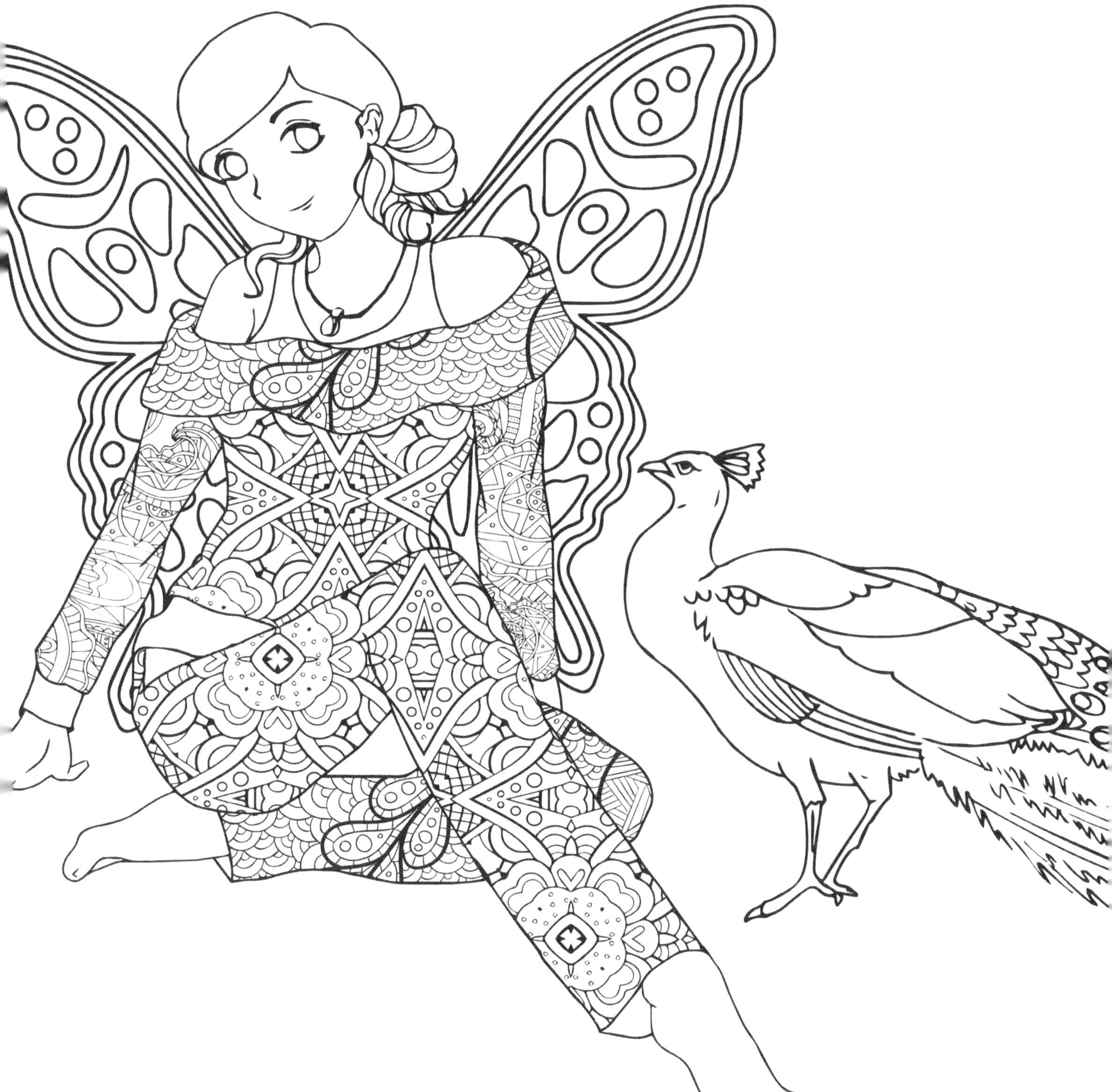

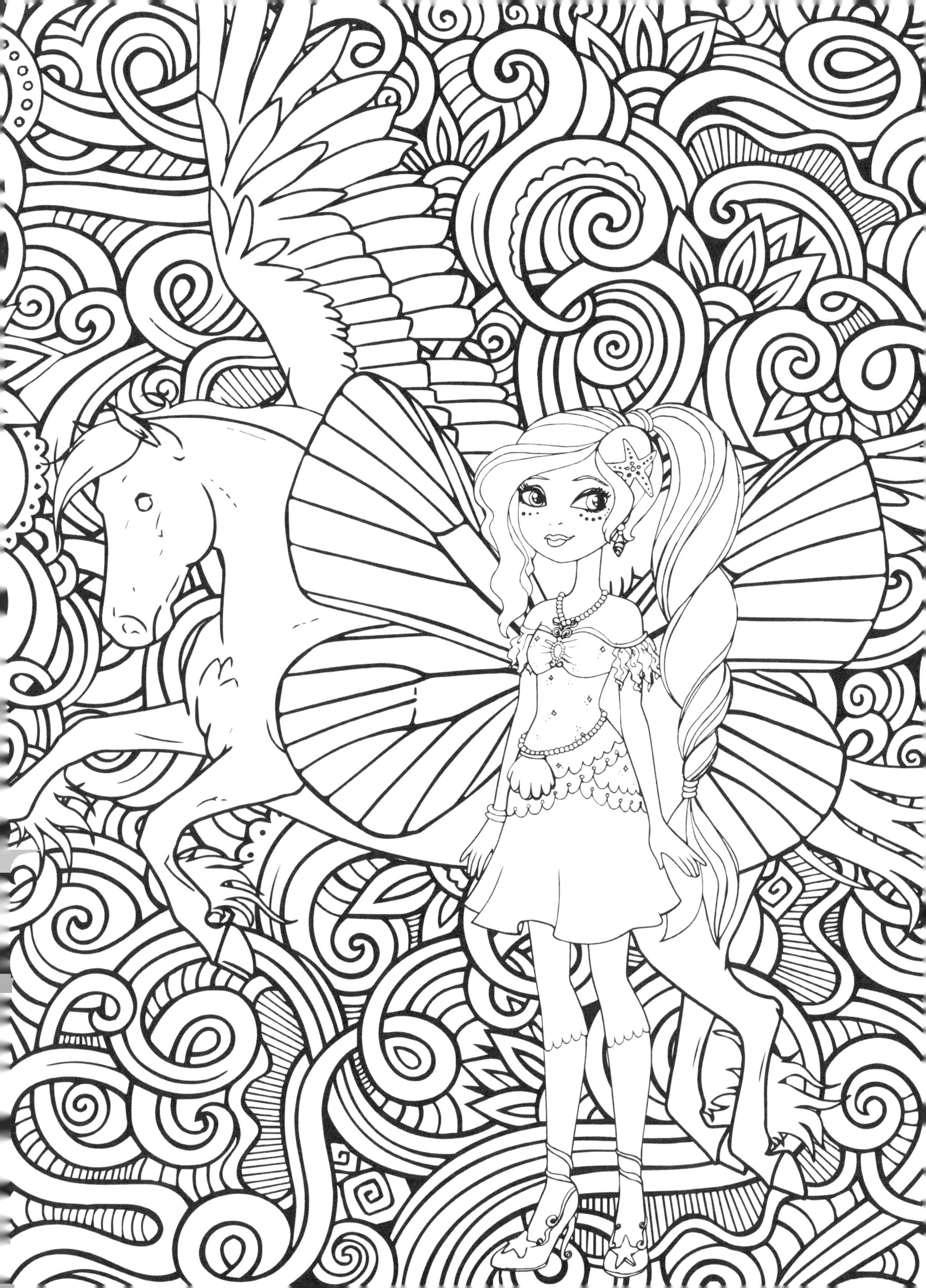

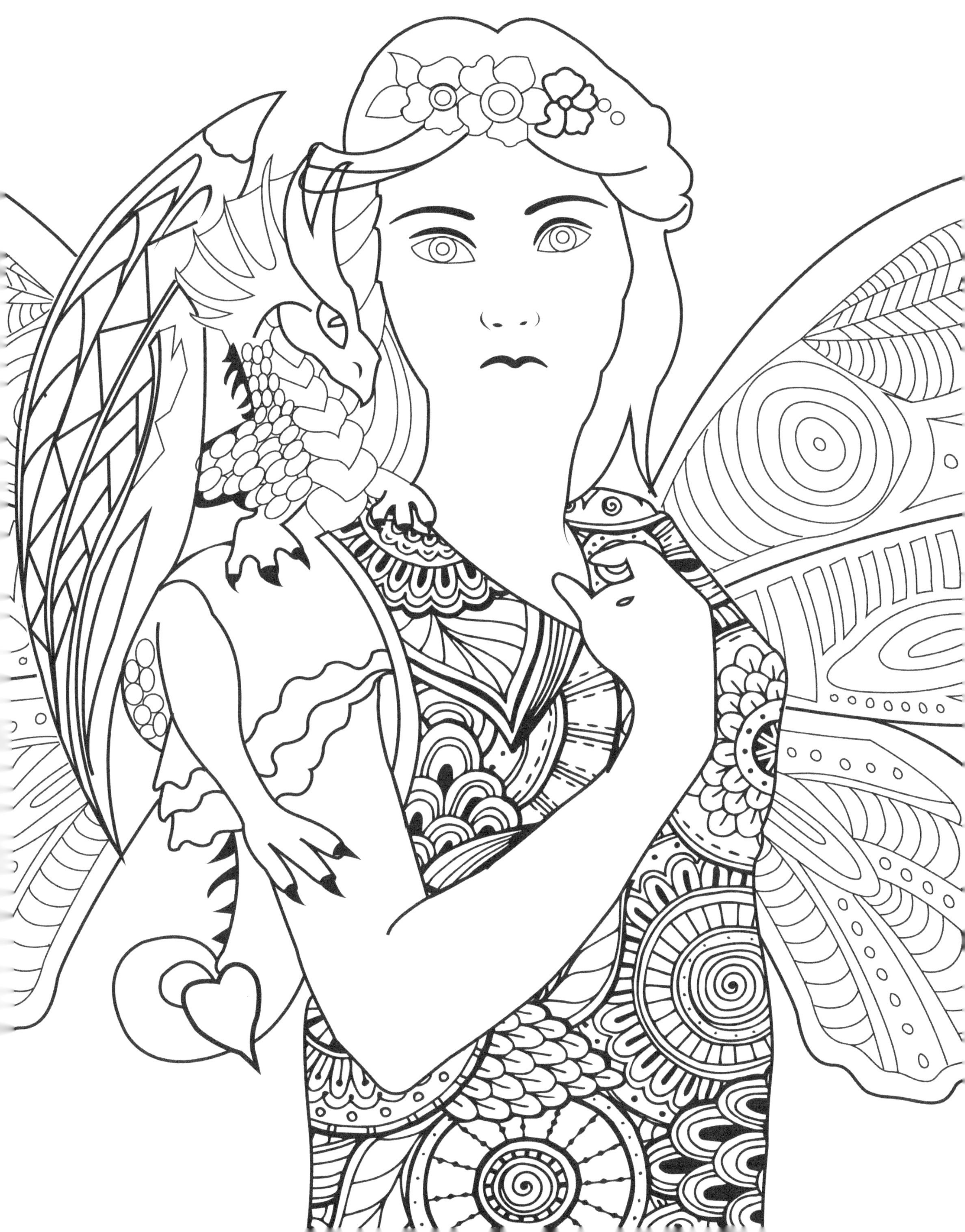

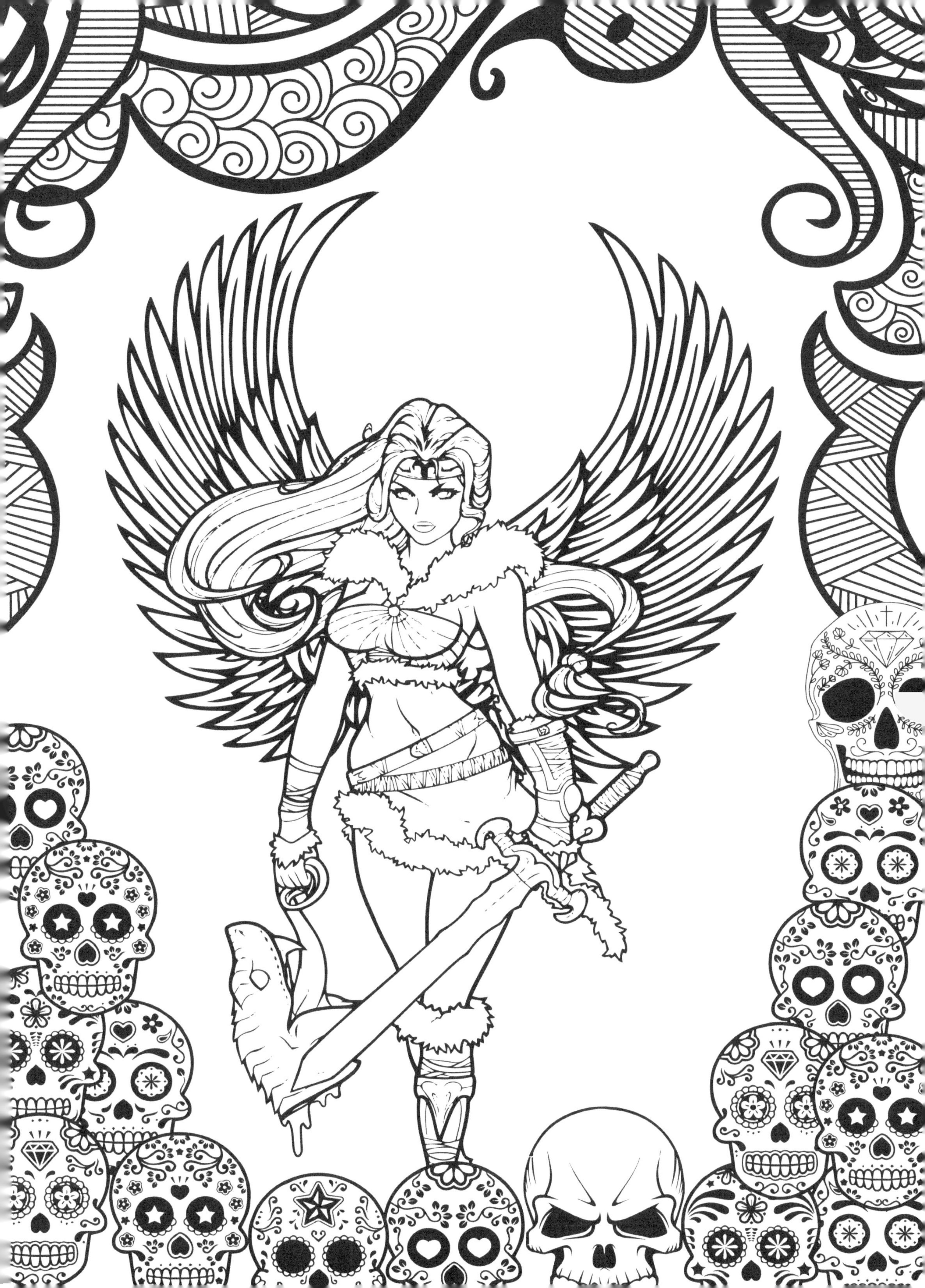

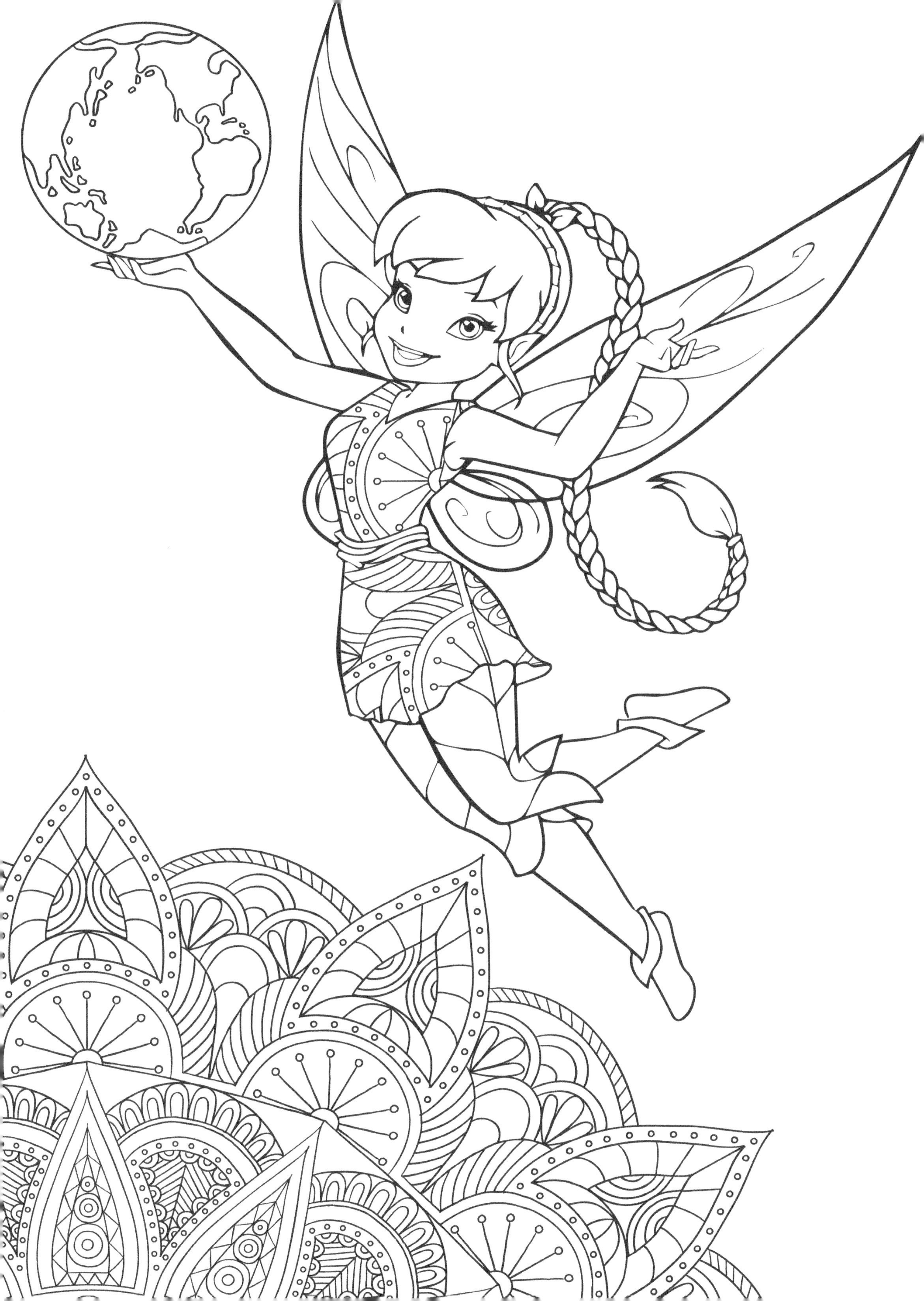

More in the Adult Coloring Book series...

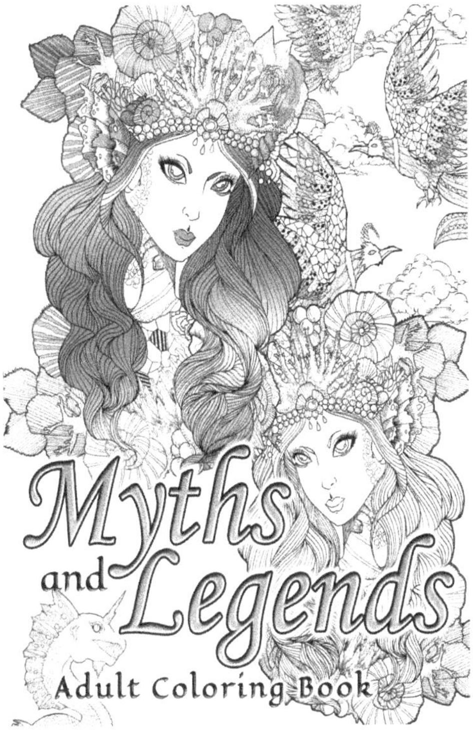

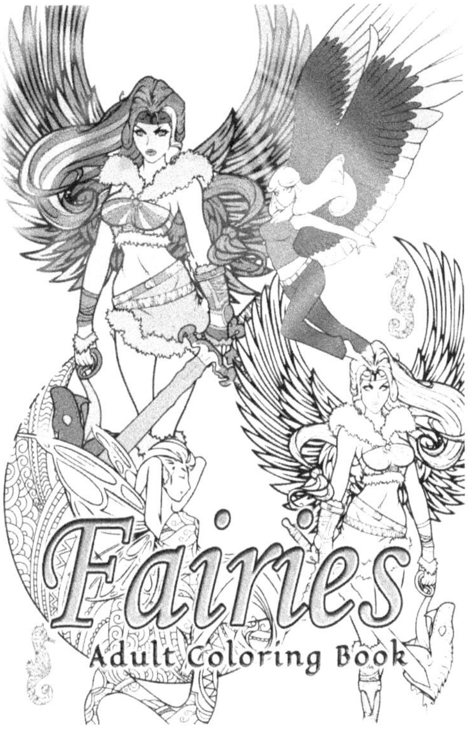

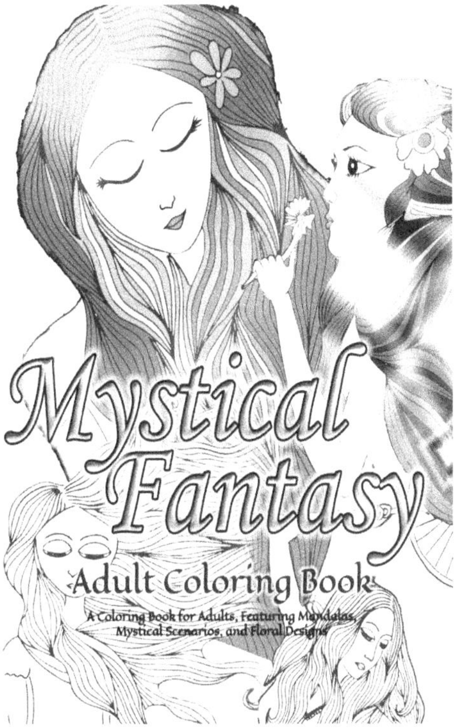

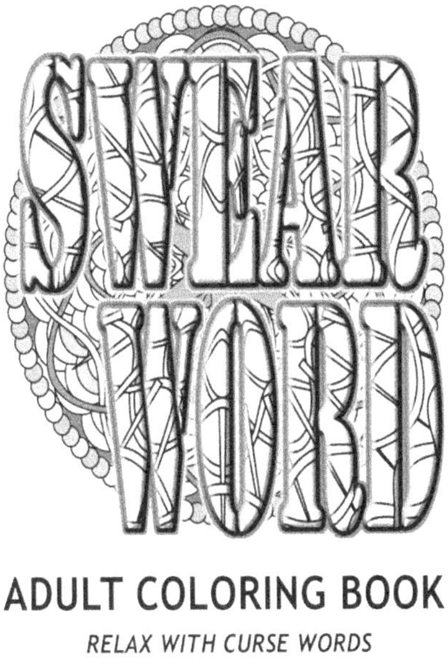

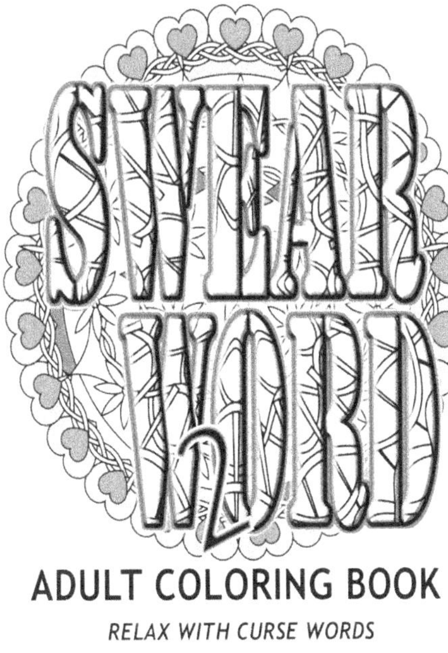

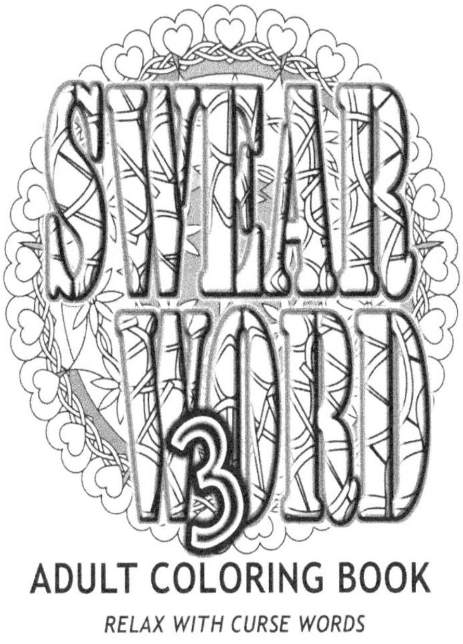

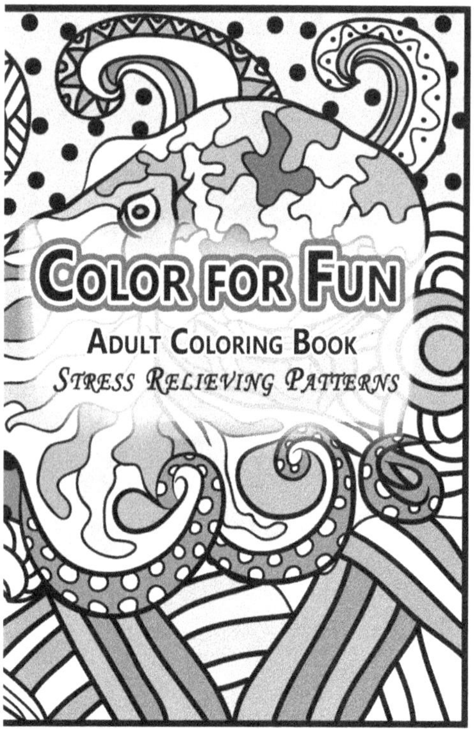
COLOR FOR FUN
ADULT COLORING BOOK
STRESS RELIEVING PATTERNS

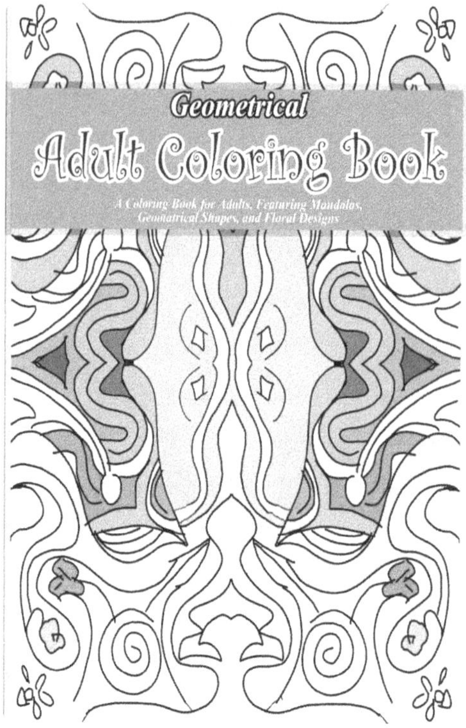
Geometrical
Adult Coloring Book
A Coloring Book for Adults, Featuring Mandalas,
Geomatrical Shapes, and Floral Designs

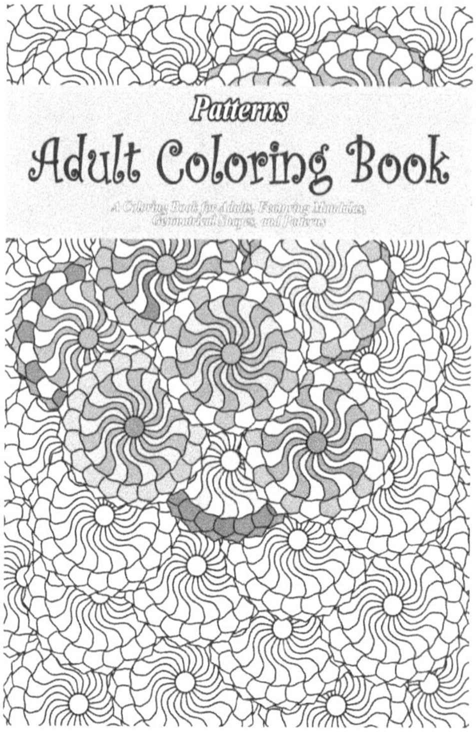
Patterns
Adult Coloring Book

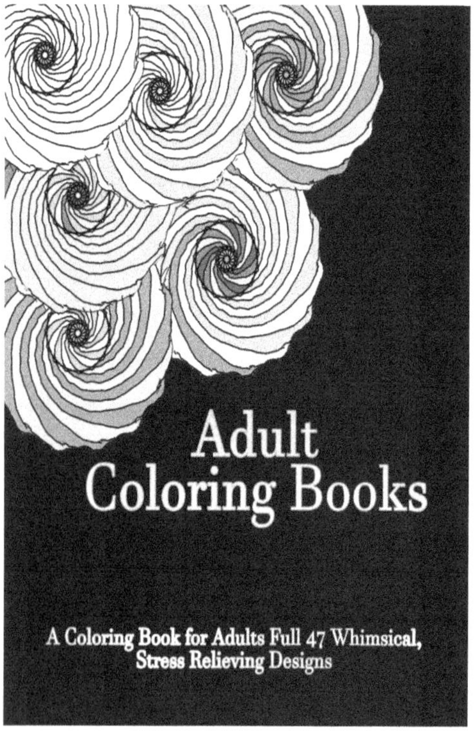
Adult
Coloring Books
A Coloring Book for Adults Full 47 Whimsical,
Stress Relieving Designs

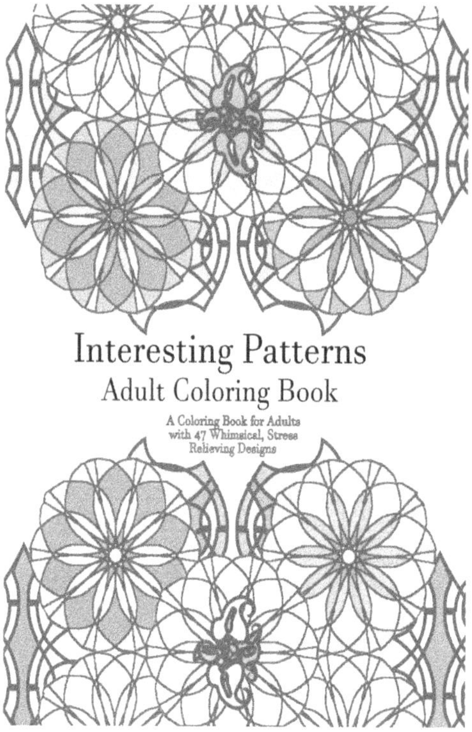
Interesting Patterns
Adult Coloring Book
A Coloring Book for Adults
with 47 Whimsical, Stress
Relieving Designs

www.ingramcontent.com/pod-product-compliance
Lightning Source LLC
Chambersburg PA
CBHW080537190526
45169CB00007B/2527
9781532827631